ROCK YOUR TRAVEL

Fly **FIRST CLASS**
Stay in **FIVE-STAR HOTELS**
and
Travel in **LUXURY**
for practically **NOTHING**

Published by Expert Message Group, LLC

Expert Message Group, LLC
P.O. Box 949
Tulsa, OK 74101

415.523.0404

www.expertmessagegroup.com

First Printing, 2013

ISBN 978-1-936875-09-2

Printed in the United States of America
Cover Design by Scott Williams
Set in Baskerville 10.5/15

WARNING

THE INFORMATION CONTAINED IN THIS BOOK WILL RESULT IN LUXURY TRAVELING TO EXOTIC LOCATIONS AT A FRACTION OF NORMAL COST, CAUSING ALL YOUR FRIENDS, FAMILY, AND CO-WORKERS TO REGARD YOU WITH ADMIRATION AND ENVY.

In this book you will learn the techniques I have used to:
- Fly my girlfriend and myself to Tokyo, Japan, in First Class (normal cost: $15,000 USD) for $105 USD.
- Stay in luxury hotels around the world for free.
- Relax while waiting for my plane in exclusive airport luxury lounges around the world with free food, free drinks (including alcohol), free Wi-Fi, private bathrooms, and even showers!
- Get upgraded to suites at hotels around the world while paying the cheapest available rate.

You will also learn:
- How a family of four flew to Hawaii for just $80.
- How to earn enough Frequent Flyer miles in one afternoon to fly from the U.S. to Europe or Asia twice in Business Class or four times in Coach.
- How to stay in a $500+ USD hotel room for $150 USD per night.
- How to reach Elite Status five times faster, allowing you to skip the long check-in and security lines at the airport and go directly to the much shorter First Class/Business line.
- How to parlay your Elite Status on one airline to another without flying a single mile.
- How to fly to Hawaii for almost 50% off every year.

Yeah, that trip of a lifetime that you've been dreaming about for way too long can finally become a reality. Then your friends will all want to know how you did it and you can tell them you learned everything you know from this book. But don't loan them your copy. Make them buy their own. It will be the best $16.95 they've ever spent. Besides, I've gotta eat.

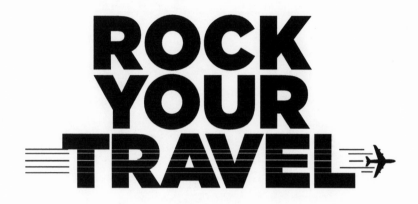

ROCK YOUR TRAVEL

Algis Tamosaitis
with Adrienne Lusby

Expert Message Group Press

Tulsa, OK

In loving memory of my mother,
Irena Tamosaitis.

FREE COMPANION ITEMS

Free companion items to this book are available at:

www.rockyourtravel.com

Contents

Part 1: Prelude to an Adventure **17**

Prologue: The Gift of Travel 19

Chapter 1: Dream Big.. 25

Chapter 2: West Meets East............................... 29

Part 2: Freedom through Frequent Flyer Miles **33**

Chapter 3: The Key to Unlocking Limitless Travel... 35

Chapter 4: Everyday Life 39

Chapter 5: Flying.. 47

Chapter 6: Credit Cards....................................... 57

Chapter 7: Becoming a Miles Millionaire..................... 67

Part 3: Flying Like a Rock Star **77**

Chapter 8: Booking Flights 79

Chapter 9: Multiple Cities for the Price of One Award:
Stopovers, Open-Jaws, and Free One-Ways

.... 89

Part 4: Travel Better **93**

Chapter 10: Elite Status.. 95

Chapter 11: Airline Lounges 105

Chapter 12: Some Expert Advice 111

Part 5: Rock Star Travel Accommodations 137

Chapter 13: Where You Stay Matters............................139

Chapter 14: Booking a Hotel Room...............................153

Part 6: Superstar Techniques **163**

Chapter 15: Pro Travel Strategies..................................165

Chapter 16: A Few Final Thoughts 177

Acknowledgements 179

Resources...181

Glossary 183

PART 1
Prelude to an Adventure

PROLOGUE

The Gift of Travel

"Life is either a daring adventure or nothing."
—Helen Keller

'm standing less than ten feet away from a pride of lions in Tanzania and trying not to lose my breath. Every move they make causes their sinewy muscles to ripple, revealing the untamed power they possess. No amount of watching *Animal Planet* could have prepared me for being this close to such beautiful and dangerous predators.

The Four Runner I'm in has areas that are completely open. A lion or leopard or cheetah could, theoretically, climb right in. I mean, they're only a few feet away as it is, and hey, maybe they're hungry? I ask the driver/guide about this possibility and he explains that the animals view our vehicle as one big animal, not as a lunch box with a bunch of tasty treats inside as I'd previously thought. He clarifies that, should I decide to step outside the vehicle, I will no longer be seen as part of this huge Four Runner animal, and will simply become lunch. *Hmmm.* Good to know. I wasn't planning on going outside with the lions anyway.

After this reassuring talk, he proceeds to tell me that sometimes the cheetahs like to climb on the hood of the car and lounge there, right by the opening where I'm standing. Not sure if he's messing with me or not, but he doesn't seem too concerned.

Going on an African Safari and witnessing these amazing creatures in their natural habitat is nothing short of awe-inspiring. Elephants charging through the brush, giraffes grazing gracefully among the trees, pods of hippos bathing themselves, and now these lions lounging about on the great savannah like they've done for thousands of years.

The irony is that I might never have ventured here if it weren't for the one person who inspired me to travel in the first place—my mother. As a child during WWII, my mother fled Lithuania with her family to escape the brutal battles over her homeland by both the Germans and Russians. Many years later, she met my father (also a Lithuanian transplant) in Australia. They fell in love, got married, and eventually moved to the U.S.

Although I was born and raised in Los Angeles, California, my household was distinctly Lithuanian. English and Lithuanian were spoken interchangeably and Lithuanian culture was as natural to me as baseball and apple pie. My parents each spoke several other languages as well (most often when they didn't want me to know what they were saying). When I was a child, they told me stories of the places they had been and the multiple lives they had led before coming to the States and it made me keenly aware that the location into which I was born would never dictate what country I might later feel was meant to be my home.

This comfort with the idea of living in other places was only enhanced by the fact that my mom was a travel agent. She would often be gone for a week at a time on an exciting trip to learn about some new country, while I would be forced to endure my father's cooking. Fortunately, my father didn't like his own cooking either, so we ate out—a lot.

Over the summers, my mother used up a great deal of my vacation time taking me to the World Trade Center in downtown Los Angeles, where I would hang out at the agency where she worked—Jesson Travel. Although I complained about not getting to play with my friends, this journey did come with a few perks. I was allowed to eat at a Japanese restaurant that I loved. All manner of atlases, brochures, and photo books on travel were available for my perusal. And, on occasion, if I was lucky, I got to hear some hard-to-believe travel stories from the agency owner, the always eccentric and entertaining Herman Jesson. With his confident grin and natural charm, he encapsulated the essence of Ernest Hemingway. What's more, he often dressed as if he was about to walk straight into the Amazonian Rain Forest that he was always so fond of.

Mr. Jesson showed me photographs of his pet kinkajou—a furry, exotic creature that looked like a cross between a monkey and a lemur—and regaled me with detailed narratives about his various adventures in South America, which often included canoeing the Amazon River. After all, he was a member of the Adventurers' Club.

The story I was never quite sure whether to believe or not, was about the Peruvian island that he owned on the Amazon River, and his interactions with the natives that lived there. Even after seeing photos of him with the native people of the island, which apparently he named "Jessonia," I would always ask my Mom if it was even possible to own an island. I never got any concrete answers. It was only years later, with the advent of the Internet, that I discovered it was indeed, all true.

Going with my Mom to the travel agency was just the tip of the iceberg. My parents didn't have the fanciest cars or the biggest house, but they did have a passion for travel and my mother made sure they shared as much of it as possible with me. By the time I was 12 years old, I had hiked the majestic Swiss Alps, swam in the aqua blue waters off the white sand beaches of Samoa, tasted the incredible, sweet flavor of fresh wild strawberries at a farmer's market on a Paris side street, slept in a small thatched bungalow in Fiji, fed koalas in Australia, and visited legendary castles in Germany.

It wasn't until years later that I realized that by exposing me to things I would have otherwise only read about in books, my mother had essentially given me the world and at the same time instilled in me a great love for travel.

A Turning Point

When my mother developed cancer in 1999, there was no question I would take care of her. My father had health issues of his own, so I became my mother's primary caretaker. We were extraordinarily close, and seeing her fall ill with such a cruel disease was truly heartbreaking on every level.

After two long years of caring for her and watching her suffer while battling her illness, she passed in the summer of 2001. Her pain was over, but my father's had only just begun. During the two years of my mother's illness, my father's health had taken several turns for the worse and so I transitioned from caring for my mother, to doing the same for my father.

After years of dialysis, my father finally received a kidney transplant. Ostensibly, this made things easier, except he would often succumb to the flu, bladder infections, and nausea. As his health deteriorated, he developed Parkinson's disease, then Ankylosing-Spondylitis (a condition that causes your spine to fuse into a single column), and eventually lung cancer. I cared for him until he passed away in the fall of 2006.

Watching my parents become less capable and less competent as they were slowly overtaken by disease at the end of life was a powerful wake-up call for me. No more putting off things I wanted to do. "Now" was all I had, all anyone had, and I was going to enjoy mine to the fullest.

So while some of my friends were buying furniture at Ikea, I was eating the world's best sushi in Japan. While others were getting loans to buy houses, I was exploring the cafes and bars of Melbourne, Australia. And while most of the people I knew were advancing in their careers, I was exploring the beaches of Thailand and photographing lions and giraffes on a safari in Africa.

Our culture naturally makes us desire things: houses, cars, fancy clothes, etc. But what do we remember most fondly? Experiences. Sights. Sounds. Smells. Feelings. This is the essence of travel.

Traveling the world deepened my respect and admiration for other countries, exotic foods, and unique cultures. It made me realize that of all the things in life I could do, the thrill and excitement of exploring new places was a priceless gift that would stay with me for the rest of my life.

CHAPTER 1

Dream Big

*"It's the possibility of having a dream come
true that makes life interesting."*
—Paulo Coelho, The Alchemist

I n 2012, a national survey asked 2000 Brits what their biggest regrets in life were. Out of the top 10 answers, "Not seeing more of the world" ranked number 4. Of all the regrets we may have in life, not seeing the world (because you thought it was too expensive) doesn't have to be one of them anymore.

Think back for a moment, to when you were a kid and anything seemed possible. What kind of adventures did you envision? Treasure hunting like Indiana Jones? Climbing Mt. Everest like Sir Edmund Hillary?

Choose three destinations and/or activities that you would consider the experiences of a lifetime. Don't limit yourself or worry about how you're going to do it. There are plenty of techniques in this book to help you get there. This is your opportunity to dream big. No one is questioning your love for your relatives, but if flying to Nebraska to visit your Grandma isn't number one on your list, don't put it there out of obligation. This is about you.

Whether it's an adventure you thought of as some long ago dream or that vacation with your family you've been talking about for years, write it down. If you're having trouble coming up with stuff, here's some suggestions to get you thinking:

- Surprise your sweetheart with a romantic trip to Paris.
- Experience the adventure of a safari in Africa.
- Test your courage by running with the bulls in Pamplona.
- Bond with your family on a ski trip to Austria.
- Learn how to surf at Australia's Noosa Beach.
- Fulfill your inner Mario Andretti by driving the Autobahn in Berlin.
- Enrich your spiritual path by practicing yoga in India.
- Tap into your artistic side in the Netherlands by oil painting during tulip season.
- Satisfy your thirst for the world's best Scotch in Scotland (they have Scotch that isn't even available for export).
- Tune out the modern world in an over-water bungalow in Fiji.
- Connect with your roots on a family trip to Ireland.
- Experience *la dolce vita* by learning to cook Italian food in Florence.
- Develop your inner bad-ass by learning jiu-jitsu in Rio de Janeiro.
- Stop and smell the flowers by enjoying cherry blossom season in Japan.
- Channel James Bond and play poker in Monte Carlo.
- Go back in time at the Colosseum in Rome.
- Take an adventure under the sea by scuba diving in the Bahamas.

Use this page to write down your travel goals, and I will help you achieve them.

_____

_____

_____

_____

_____

_____

_____

_____

_____

_____

_____

_____

_____

_____

_____

_____

_____

_____

_____

_____

_____

_____

_____

How to Use This Book

There are tons of travel guidebooks out there that recommend places to go, sites to see, and things to experience once you've arrived at the destination of your choice. These books are great. I've purchased many of them myself and poured over their pages, thinking about all the cool things I'd want to do in Rome or Tokyo or Sydney. However, the problem with these guidebooks is there's one thing they don't mention, and that's how to get there in the first place.

The tips, tricks, and secrets in this book will help you understand the system, save you money, and allow you to travel in style for practically nothing. They will unlock the door to exotic locations, bustling cities, and serene beaches.

Once you begin practicing these techniques, you'll begin looking at travel magazines as catalogues filled with exciting possibilities rather than photos of the impossible. You won't have to wait until the end of the book to learn about the key strategies I use for traveling the world in style. However, I suggest reading the book all the way through first to get an idea of all the travel possibilities available to you. Then you can decide which strategies are best for you and begin planning your dream vacation.

You don't need to learn and remember everything all at once. Once you understand the big ideas, you can use this book again and again as a reference when you plan your trips. You can also find more resources, travel inspiration and new updates at: rockyourtravel.com

CHAPTER 2

West Meets East

*"May all your trails be crooked, winding, lonesome,
dangerous, leading to the most amazing view, where
something strange and more beautiful and more full of
wonder than your deepest dreams waits for you."*
—Edward Abbey

Flying to Tokyo for the Price of a Steak Dinner

My girlfriend and I have been enjoying a luxurious morning in our room some 30 floors up at the Four-Star Hilton Tokyo Hotel. We awoke to the incredible view of Shinjuku on a clear sunny day and although our stylish room, the indoor pool, rooftop tennis courts, and a multitude of fantastic restaurants are a constant reminder that staying in one of Tokyo's best hotels absolutely free (using points) certainly has its perks, I can hardly wait to whisk us out of the hotel to roam through my favorite city in the world.

Japan is a country where the hyper-modern coexists with a deep reverence for centuries-old tradition. The love of Western culture co-mingles with Japanese attitudes.

I've been to Japan many times and I never tire of it. Recently, I had the pleasure of taking my girlfriend there—twice; the first time in Business Class and the second time, in First Class.

Both trips were fantastic. But flying First Class for $52.50 each was really spectacular. An 11-hour flight in Coach can only be described as grueling, but in First Class it's a whole different world. We were treated to tasty food, wine, freshly-baked cookies (yes they bake them on the plane) and for dessert ... hot fudge sundaes (all FREE). Then we changed into our cozy complimentary pajamas to watch movies on our private movie screens. When we got tired, our cushy chairs turned into lay-flat beds, made up by the flight attendants with down comforters to boot. We slipped on our eye masks (provided along with other goodies in our free amenity kits) and slept to our hearts' content. When we awoke, we had the option to order more food and drinks on the menu and enjoy the rest of our flight before landing. Despite the long flight to our destination, we arrived at our hotel in Japan well fed, well rested, and ready for all Tokyo has to offer.

Eating the freshest sushi for breakfast at Tsukiji Fish Market, shopping at the world's largest Uniqlo store in Ginza, experiencing the grandeur and power of the giant Buddha in Kamakura, seeing the Harajuku girls and Goth-Lolitas wander around in "costume," posing for cameras, and savoring grilled delicacies while enjoying the strange Blade Runner atmosphere of Yakitori Alley. There are so many amazing things to do that I couldn't possibly list them all. Tokyo is filled with once-in-a-lifetime experiences ... but you have to get here first.

So by now you are probably wondering how my girlfriend and I could possibly fly round trip from L.A. to Tokyo in First Class for only $105.

Simple: By using Frequent Flyer (FF) miles we earned quickly and easily. To be clear, we used FF miles to purchase our tickets for free. The $105 was for the airport and government fees.

There are a multitude of tricks and secrets on how to play the travel game in this book, but plain and simple, earning FF miles is your key to limitless travel.

As you may have guessed, the more FF miles you have, the better you can travel. In the next several chapters, I will outline the multitude of easy ways to earn FF miles as well as the single most powerful way to get all the miles you need to take your dream trip now.

Becoming a RST (Rock Star Traveler) is a key lifestyle change ...*waaay* more exciting than that trip to Target you were planning on taking later today. So get in the game, start learning, and start earning.

PART 2

Freedom through Frequent Flyer Miles

CHAPTER 3

The Key to Unlocking Limitless Travel

*"Live! Life is a banquet and most poor suckers
are starving to death!"*
—Auntie Mame

'm hanging out with a group of people at a bar in Melbourne, when the conversation turns to travel. One of the women in the group mentions that she's visiting from New York and is heading back home in a week. I ask her which airline she flew and if she was signed up for their FF program. She tells me she doesn't fly often, so she never bothered signing up for a FF account. Still reeling from her oversight, I tell her she would have earned enough miles from this trip alone for a free domestic flight in the U.S.

She's impressed, and proceeds to ask me where I'm staying ... *which is the precise moment I realize the seductive power of Frequent Flyer Miles.*

Melbourne, Australia

Now that you've started fantasizing about secluded white sand beaches with warm water, an endless supply of perfect lefts, impossible sunsets to be savored with friends, and freshly made Mai Tai's, let's talk about earning the miles to get you there. You can't be a RST (Rock Star Traveler) when you're freezing your butt off in Wisconsin. No offense, Wisconsinites—Madison is a beautiful city, but damn it's cold. Get thee to a tropical beach!

There are tons of opportunities to earn FF miles these days. The good thing is most of them are for things that you already do. I mean do you eat out at restaurants? Do you buy stuff? Clothes? TVs? Vitamins for your fitness obsession? Flowers for your mom on Mother's Day? Do you use a credit card? Netflix? You can earn FF miles for all of these things. And you *should*. These days there's almost nothing you can't earn miles for.

Airlines have some pretty cool (FF) loyalty programs, but they're not going out of their way to tell you to sign up for them. If you travel, plan to travel, or think you might someday like to travel, signing up for the right FF program is your first step to earning tons of FF miles well before you even step on a plane. Then you can use those miles you earn instead of cash to fly in First/Business Class for less than your friends spend to fly Coach and stay in fancy hotels all over the world for free.

Signing up for airline FF programs is absolutely free, so there's no reason to hold back on signing up for as many airline FF programs as you choose. Later I will break down the various FF programs to help you decide which program(s) are best for you. But first, lets learn a little bit more about how these programs can help you on your way to becoming a RST.

Earning Miles Without Even Trying

A few of the ways airline FF programs allow you to earn miles right away are:

- Flying with that airline or one of its partners.
- Shopping through the airline's online shopping portal.
- And the fastest way: Applying for a mileage-earning credit card to quickly and easily receive a huge FF mile sign-up bonus.

There are numerous other ways to earn miles without even stepping on a plane. But we'll get to that a little later. After earning enough miles, you can book "free" (also known as "award") tickets.

There are three basic categories of mileage earning:

EVERYDAY LIFE, FLYING, and **CREDIT CARDS**

A lot of Frequent Flyer aficionados like to joke that Frequent Flyer programs have become frequent *buyer* programs because you can earn staggering amounts of miles this way.

CHAPTER 4

Everyday Life

"We live in a wonderful world that is full of beauty, charm, and adventure. There is no end to the adventures we can have if only we seek them with our eyes open."
—Jawaharial Nehru

M y friend Paul is a health and fitness guy. He shops at Whole Foods, and takes vitamin and protein supplements. Perhaps you know someone like this.

He's a relatively smart guy, but what Paul doesn't know is, if he did those things just slightly differently, he could easily earn one free Domestic Award Ticket every year, just for being a slightly more informed version of himself.

Let me break this down:

Miles Earned from Paul's Food Purchases

The $1,000 USD he spends per month on food for himself and his girlfriend (they live together) at Whole Foods would earn him a minimum of 1,000 FF miles per month if he just paid his bill with an airline co-branded credit card.

That's **12,000 FF miles** per year.

Miles Earned from Paul's Supplement Purchases

The $200 USD he spends on supplements could earn him 8 miles per dollar spent if he purchased them via an online Airline Mileage Mall instead of at the local vitamin store. That's 1,600 FF miles per month plus 200 FF miles for using an airline co-branded credit card to pay for them.

So, 1,800 FF miles x 12 months equals **21,600 FF miles per year.**

Paul's food shopping and supplement purchases could earn him **33,600 FF miles per year**. Domestic round-trip awards are only 25,000 FF miles, so these two things alone would be enough for a round-trip Domestic Award Flight with 8,600 miles to spare. By purchasing items he was already buying, in a different way, he'd be earning this many miles *every single year*.

Airline Mileage Malls

Most major U.S. airlines (American, United, U.S. Airways, Delta, etc.) and even some smaller ones (Hawaiian Airlines) have Mileage Shopping Malls. All you have to do is sign up. It doesn't cost you anything.

Remember, first you need to sign up for that airline's Mileage Program. Then, when you're ready to make that big purchase (MacBook Air anyone?), you just go to the Airline's Shopping Portal and find stores that sell it and see how many bonus miles they are offering. (**Note:** You can find direct links to all the major mileage malls at: rockyourtravel.com)

The malls contain tons of online retailers. A quick perusal of American Airlines eShopping Mall reveals some very popular brands like Nordstrom, Apple, Target, Best Buy, Home Depot, and REI, to name just a few.

Most companies offer 3 FF miles per dollar spent but some are more generous. Here are just a few examples:

- Eddie Bauer offers 6 FF miles per dollar spent.
- GNC offers 8 FF miles per dollar spent.
- Rosetta Stone offers 8 FF miles per dollar spent.
- ValueMags offers 23 FF miles per dollar spent.

These miles can add up very quickly. Let's say I wanted to buy a new MacBook Air. They cost around $1500. Buy.com (via AA eShopping Mall) is offering 3 FF miles per dollar spent. So if I purchase the MacBook Air through them, I will receive **4,500 FF miles**. Plus, if I use my airline miles credit card, which gives me 1 mile per dollar spent, then I will earn an additional 1,500 FF miles. That's a grand total of 6,000 FF miles earned in one easy transaction for something I was going to buy anyway! You can do this with many big-ticket items (computer, TV, camera, video camera, etc.).

Buying stuff you normally buy on a monthly basis is another consistent way to add FF miles to your account. In addition to traditional purchases, you can even buy gift cards via the mileage mall. So when birthdays and holidays roll around, order your gift cards via the airline portal and get rewarded with more miles. Whether it's gifts or gift cards, just imagine how many miles a family of four could rack up at Christmas time alone.

Airline Mileage Dining Programs

I don't know about you, but I love to eat. A lot. Often. Practically every day. So when I found out you could earn extra airline miles just by eating at certain restaurants, I was all over this.

Airline Mileage Dining Programs are a great way to earn extra miles for your upcoming travel. Let me break this down for you.

- It is FREE to sign up and only takes a few minutes online to do so.

- You don't need an airline miles credit card to sign up. You can link ANY credit or debit card to a mileage-dining program. Although, as you'll see later, airline miles cards are the superhighway to free flights.

- Most programs give you a sign-up bonus of between 500 FF miles and 1000 FF miles after your first dining experience at a partner restaurant of over $25. That's in addition to what you earn for eating at that restaurant.

- When you dine at participating restaurants, bars, and clubs, you receive 3-5 FF miles per dollar spent, depending on your status level, which is determined by how many times you've dined at participating restaurants. For example, in the Alaska Airlines program, it takes 12 dines to reach the 5 FF miles per dollar level.

- You earn miles on your entire bill: food, drinks, tax, and tip.

- There are restaurants, bars, and clubs. Who knew having some drinks at one of your local spots could earn so many miles so quickly?

- Also, you don't need to inform the server or present a membership card or anything like that. The program is linked to the credit card or debit card of your choice, so no one knows you are getting all those bonus miles but you. All you have to do is pay with the card you signed up with.

Dining programs often run special promotions that increase the number of miles you can earn. In the past, they've had promotions for double miles on Mon., Tues., and Wed. dines, provided you filled out a quick online questionnaire within 30 days of dining at the restaurant. So depending on your status, that's 6-10 miles per dollar spent.

Before you assume that only mediocre restaurants participate in these programs, let me assure you that is not the case. There are tons of restaurants listed that range from super-cheap to super-chic. You can check online and your dining program will list all the restaurants near you, so you can make a delicious decision.

It's true that if you are in a smaller city, the number of participating places can be considerably less, but it's still worth signing up, as you are likely to travel to cities that have participating restaurants. On my recent visit to D.C., I accidentally ate at two participating restaurants and only found out when I saw my monthly miles reward statement. It's cool to get extra miles for going to places that you would normally go to anyway.

Since it's free to join, you can join multiple programs if you want, but you can only register a card for one program at a time. They don't let you double dip. This is easy to get around though. For example, just register one credit card with United and a different card with American. Choose the programs that work best for you.

To find links to the sign-up pages for all the Airline Dining Programs just go to: rockyourtravel.com.

So while your friends are discussing politics, you can be thinking about the Tahitian beach you will soon be luxuriating on RST style, with all the airline miles you are earning from choosing the bar in your program instead of the one next door.

Car Rentals

Renting a car is another way to earn airline miles. All the car rental companies have partnerships with the airlines. Just make sure to provide them with your FF# when you rent.

Hotel Stays

Hotels have their own loyalty programs. You can also opt to earn airline miles instead of hotel points when you stay at a hotel, and some hotels (Hilton, for example) allow you to double dip and earn BOTH hotel points and FF miles.

Booking a Cruise or Vacation

All the major airlines have cruise and vacation booking departments with promotions that offer various package deals: flight, hotel, car rental combos, and the like. If you book through them you can receive bonus miles.

Financial/Banking Services

Investing companies TD Ameritrade and Fidelity often offer mileage bonuses for using their services. It's worth checking your FF program "earn miles" tab and looking under "financial" to see what current offers are available. Past offers have been for as much as 50,000 airline miles!

Mortgages

If you're in the market for a new home, you can earn miles by financing with a company that has an agreement with your FF airline. You can find this information by going to your airline's website and searching through the FF program's info on earning miles.

Netflix

Sign up for Netflix and earn 2,000 United miles.

Note: These offers change often. The above offers were accurate at the time of publication of this book.

Buying Miles

Yes, you can even buy miles. I know this sounds weird, but sometimes you only need a small amount of miles to reach an award. If you want to go to Europe, which requires a 50,000 mile award ticket, and you only have 48,000 miles, it could be well worth it to buy those last 2,000 miles and then go ahead and book the Award ticket instead of waiting to earn those 2,000 miles some other way. Buying 2,000 miles on American Airlines (including fees and taxes) only costs around $100 *not* $2,000 dollars!

(Later I'll explain how to use a "buying miles" technique to fly First Class for 80% off.)

Preventing Your Miles from Expiring

IMPORTANT: Most FF miles will expire if your account has no activity!

Most FF miles expire somewhere between 18 months and two years after you earn them if there is no activity in the account. What?! That sucks! Yes, it does. However, it's easy to prevent miles from expiring. You simply need to **use some or earn some** and then the expiration date moves 18-24 months into the future depending on the program.

Some easy ways to keep your miles alive:

- Eat at a restaurant that participates in your Mileage-Dining Program.
- Shop through your airline's mileage-earning portal.
- Use a mileage-earning credit card.
- Book an Award flight using some of your miles.

Also, websites like AwardWallet.com will actually let you know ahead of time which miles are set to expire.

Where Are Those Bonus Miles Opportunities, Again?

Go to your main airline's FF program and look through the various ways to earn bonus miles. As you've seen from the examples above, there are things you already do and use that could be earning you miles.

CHAPTER 5
Flying

*"If birds can glide for long periods of time, then...
why can't I?"*
—*Orville Wright*

The most obvious way you can earn miles is from flying on an airplane. Shocking, I know. At the most basic level, you'll earn: 1 FF mile per mile flown. So if you fly 1000 miles you earn 1000 FF miles.

Of course, you'll only earn these miles if you have a FF account and give the airline your FF number when you book your flight. The airlines don't keep track of your flights for you and magically add your FF number when you fly somewhere. You ***must*** enter your number online when you book the ticket or at check-in so they can input your FF number into the system.

With a little basic math you can sort out how quickly you will be earning free flights from flying.

If you fly round-trip from L.A. to N.Y., you'll earn approximately: 5,000 FF miles.

An award redemption for a domestic flight is: 25,000 FF miles.

Therefore, five round-trip flights between L.A. and NY will earn you: **1 FREE FLIGHT.**

In addition to earning one FF mile per mile flown, you can get bonus miles for flying First Class/Business Class instead of Coach, for taking advantage of Special Route Bonuses, and/or for having earned Elite Status. I will explain Elite Status thoroughly in Chapter 10.

Remember the woman at the bar in Melbourne? It's unfortunate she didn't sign up for a Frequent Flyer program. If she had, it would look something like this:

New York to Sydney (Via Hong Kong):
25,306 miles round-trip.

Frequent Flyer Miles she could have earned:
25,306 miles

Miles needed for a free round-trip flight in the U.S.:
25,000 miles

Miles needed for Elite Status on most U.S. carriers:
25,000 miles

If only she had taken the five minutes to sign up for a FF program, she'd have already earned a free flight *and* Elite Status.

So why didn't she?

Like many people, she simply didn't understand FF programs or how good their benefits could be.

If someone told you that spending five minutes or less filling out a couple of forms could get you a free flight, you'd probably do it, right? Becoming an RST is very easy if you're willing to put in a little time.

In addition to the 1 FF mile per mile-flown standard, there are numerous ways to earn even more miles every time you fly.

Flying First/Business Class

Yes, the rich really do get richer. When you fly First or Business Class you get mileage-earning bonuses that can range from 25% to 100% bonus miles earned! It varies by airline.

Elite Status Mileage Bonuses

When you have Elite Status, you will also receive bonuses on FF miles earned. Here's a little chart on the next page that shows the mileage earned bonuses from some of the biggest programs:

ELITE STATUS MILEAGE BONUSES

American Airlines
Gold (entry level) – 25% bonus miles earned.
Platinum (mid-level) – 100 % bonus miles earned.
Executive Platinum (top level) – 100% bonus miles earned.

United Airlines
Premier Silver (entry level) – 25% bonus miles earned.
Premier Gold (low mid-level) – 50% bonus miles earned.
Premier Platinum (high mid-level) – 75% bonus miles earned.
Premier 1k (top level) – 100% bonus miles earned.

Delta
Silver (entry level) – 25% bonus miles earned.
Gold (low mid-level) – 50% bonus miles earned.
Platinum (high mid-level) – 75% bonus miles earned.
Diamond (top level) – 100% bonus miles earned.

US Airways
Silver (entry level) – 25% bonus miles earned.
Gold (low mid-level) – 50% bonus miles earned.
Platinum (high mid-level) – 75% bonus miles earned.
Chairman's (top level) – 100% bonus miles earned.

When looking at the Elite Status Mileage Bonus Box, you will see that if you have Platinum Status on American and you fly the same route (L.A. to N.Y.) as in our previous example, you now earn 5000 miles for flying and *another* 5000 as an Elite Bonus. Now you only need **2.5 flights** (instead of 5) to earn **1 Domestic Round-Trip ticket**!

Special Route Bonuses

Airlines often award bonus FF miles for flying specific routes. These are usually new routes, but really could be any route they want more business on. The bonuses can be a Double or Triple Mile Bonus based on how many miles that route is, or a set amount of extra bonus miles not based on flight distance.

Let's look at how quickly those miles can add up.

- Base number of miles earned flying from L.A. to New York is approximately: 5,000 miles round-trip.
- With a double miles bonus you earn *another*: 5,000 miles.
- Having mid-tier Elite Status earns yet *another*: 5,000 miles.
- **So 1 round-trip from L.A. to NY now earns: 15,000 miles.**

Now only **2** round-trip flights from L.A. to New York (instead of 5) earn you a round-trip domestic ticket Award (30,000 FF miles earned. 25,000 needed). Buy two, get one free. This is getting good.

You can check the Bonus Section of any airline's website to see what specials they are running.

IMPORTANT FREQUENT FLYER FACTS AND HOW ALLIANCES CAN TAKE YOU ALL OVER THE WORLD.

Not all Airline Loyalty Programs are Created Equal.

Different airlines are better at getting you to certain places than others. It's important to know which airlines have the best award redemptions to which locations.

For example:

British Airways FF miles are awesome for short distance awards on their partner airlines because their awards are based on how many miles you fly instead of a set amount of FF miles from one region to another.

Therefore, British Airways award redemptions from the west coast of the U.S. to Hawaii are a great deal. 25,000 British Airways Avios (their name for their FF miles) plus around $20 USD will get you a round trip economy ticket to Hawaii on American Airlines or Alaska Airlines (two of their partner airlines). If you were to book the same flight directly through American Airlines, it would take 35,000-45,000 FF miles (depending on whether it's off-peak or not) and booking through Alaska Airlines would take 40,000-55,000 FF miles.

Understanding more about various FF miles will enable you to make informed decisions about which miles to collect and how best to use them for amazing travel experiences. The bonus material includes information on which miles are best for various destinations and how the routing rules of different airlines affect how much travel you can get out of your FF miles.

Which Airline has "The Best" FF Program?

There's no "best" FF program. They all have their pros and cons. You need to choose the FF program that's "best for you." In order to do that, there are several things to consider:

Your Home Airport

Consider choosing an airline that has the most flights out of your home airport. If you live in or near a hub of one of the major airlines, they will have the most options for flights. This can make your choice easier.

Here's a quick list of some hub cities:

United	Chicago, Denver, Los Angeles, San Francisco, Washington D.C.
American Airlines	Dallas/Ft. Worth, Miami, Los Angeles
Delta	Atlanta, Cincinnati
US Airways	Charlotte, Philadelphia, Pittsburgh
Alaska Airlines	Seattle

Concentrate Your Miles

You already know that to earn a domestic round-trip award ticket in the U.S., you generally need 25,000 miles. But, keep in mind those 25,000 miles need to be all in the same FF program.

FF miles from one airline's FF program **cannot** be combined with or transferred to another airline's FF program. So having five different programs with 5,000 miles in each gets you *nothing*, whereas having 25,000 in **ONE** program gets you a domestic round-trip ticket.

In addition, the average flyer can earn more miles and travel awards like Elite Status, free upgrades, and award flights much more quickly by earning their points primarily in one program.

Consider Your Travel Goals

Remember the travel goals you wrote down earlier? You need to pick an airline that will get you there. Make sure you choose an airline that flies where you want to go or has partners (see alliances below) that do.

Learn the Alliances

When you are choosing a Frequent Flyer Program, you are **not** just choosing that airline. You are choosing its partners also. Knowing your alliances is a key factor in becoming a RST. The three main airline alliances are: Star Alliance, OneWorld Alliance and SkyTeam Alliance

The box below shows which airlines belong to each alliance.

Star Alliance

Adria Airways
Aegean Airlines
Air Canada
Air China
Air New Zealand
ANA
Asiana Airlines
Austrian
Avianca
Blue 1
brussels airlines
Copa Airlines
Croatia Airlines
EGYPTAIR
Ethiopian Airlines

LOT Polish Airlines
Lufthansa
Scandinavian Airlines
Shenzhen Airlines
Singapore Airlines
South African Airways
SWISS
TAM Airlines
TAP Portugal
THAI
Turkish Airlines
United
US Airways

OneWorld Alliance

airberlin
American Airlines
British Airways
Cathay Pacific
Finnair
Iberia
Japan Airlines (JAL)

LAN
Qantas
Qatar (joining between 2013-2014)
Royal Jordanian
S7 Airlines

SkyTeam Alliance

Aeroflot
Aerolineas Argentinas
Aeromexico
Air Europa
Air France
Alitalia
China Airlines
China Eastern
China Southern

Czech Airlines
Delta Air Lines
Kenya Airways
KLM
Korean Air
MEA (Middle East Airlines)
Saudia Airlines
TAROM
Vietnam Airlines

Independent Airlines and Partners

There are various independent airlines, and one of my favorites is Alaska Airlines. Below is a list of Alaska's partners.

Alaska Airlines Partners:

Air France
Air Pacific
American Airlines
British Airways
Cathay Pacific
Delta Air Lines
Emirates
Era Alaska

Icelandair
Kenmore Air
KLM
Korean Air
LAN
PenAir
Qantas

The Benefits of Alliances

Let's take an example from the box.

If you're an American Airlines FF member and decide to fly to Spain on Iberia Airlines (one of AA's partner airlines in the OneWorld Alliance), instead of crediting your miles to Iberia, you can input your American Airlines' FF# on your Iberia reservation and credit your miles **to American Airlines instead**.

In other words, miles you fly on an airline in the *same alliance* as your main FF Airline can be credited to your main FF account. Remember, concentrate your miles to earn free travel awards faster.

Travel Awards Using Alliances

Let's say you've flown to Spain and credited your miles to your American Airlines' FF account. Maybe you flew to a few other places as well and you now have enough FF miles in your AA account for an award (aka "free") ticket. But now you want to use your FF miles for an award ticket to fly to Sydney, Australia, *a place American Airlines doesn't fly.*

No problem. By checking AA's partners in the OneWorld Alliance, you will see that Qantas is part of the OneWorld Alliance, and *they* fly to Australia. But remember, FF miles *cannot be transferred from one airline to another.*

So how do you get your free flight on Qantas?

Simple. When you search for Award Flights on the American Airlines website, you will see Qantas as the carrier on most flights to Australia. So you find the flight you want and use your American Airlines FF miles on the American Airlines website to book an award ticket on a Qantas flight. Get it? Options galore.

It pays to know your Alliances.

CHAPTER 6
Credit Cards

"When one man, for whatever reason, has the opportunity to lead an extraordinary life, he has no right to keep it to himself."
—Jacques Yves Cousteau

In the last chapter I outlined a multitude of easy ways you can earn FF miles. But if you're a fan of Pareto's Law, then you want to know which strategy provides the most impact with the least amount of time and money spent.

Whenever I talk to people about travel, they ask me what single thing they can do right away to be able to have the vacation of their dreams. My answer is always the same. The single most powerful technique for getting free travel is credit card sign-up bonuses.

Before we go any further, I want to stress that I don't want you to ever be playing fast and loose with your credit. As Dave Ramsey says in his book *The Total Money Makeover*: "Debt is not a tool." There are many other ways to earn FF miles and get free travel that are explained in the book.

In this chapter, you will learn the most efficient technique for earning FF miles. Period. This is the strategy that travel experts use to get the maximum amount of luxury travel for the minimum amount of time and money. Even better, you don't need to be an expert or travel extensively to take advantage of this tactic and immediately earn enough miles for an award ticket.

Much to the benefit of the banks, people use their credit cards every day. You probably have a few in your wallet right now. But is the card you're using benefiting you?

In order to get your business, many banks are giving away free trips in exchange for you getting their airline co-branded credit card. By applying and getting approved for the right card, you could instantly receive enough FF miles for at least one free flight!

Most airlines have an airline co-branded credit card that earns airline FF miles. But the real value is in the huge sign-up bonus you receive when you apply, get accepted, and meet that card's "minimum spend" (see gray page for "minimum spend"). By knowing which credit cards (also known as "miles cards") to apply for and then getting approved for them, you'll be well on your way to rocking your travel without ever picking up a guitar.

Seeing the world has never been easier. If you have good credit (and sometimes even if you don't) you can apply for the right cards and easily earn enough miles from sign-up bonuses to fly and stay in amazing hotels all over the world for free.

Here's how a family of four flew to Hawaii for $80.

Emiliana Dore

"My husband Patrick spent many happy vacations in Kauai when he was a kid and had always wanted to return. We talked about visiting there for years, but we kept putting it off due to financial concerns and other constraints. With both of us working middle income jobs and also being parents of two young children, a trip of that scope just always seemed a little bit beyond our means. But when we talked to Algis about all of the amazing trips that he was taking, we started to realize that there might be a way for us to achieve our dream.

Since Algis regularly keeps an eye out for great credit card deals, he was able to tell us about an amazing miles offer from British Airways. We wouldn't have considered British Airways on our own, since we assumed that they only fly to Europe, but Algis explained that many airlines partner with each other. British Airways partners with American Airlines, which has direct flights between Los Angeles and Kauai—an important consideration for us since we'd be traveling with young children.

As it turned out, we found out about the credit card offer right at the same time we had a large tax payment due. My husband and I each applied for our own British Airways credit cards and were both approved. As soon as we received the cards, we used them to pay our taxes, thereby meeting our minimum spend requirements, which gave each of us a credit of 100,000 FF miles. In our case, we had already set aside money to pay the taxes, so we were able to immediately pay the credit cards off. We're very cautious financially and would never consider going into debt to fund travel, but since we already had the money to pay off the charges immediately, this scenario worked out perfectly for us.

Using 100,000 of the FF miles we earned, we were able to book four Award Flights to Kauai (two seats for ourselves and two for our children.)

Continued on the next page ······▶

Without the miles, four non-stop flights from LAX to Kauai would have cost us around $3,000, but we were able to book all four flights for an $80 booking/tax fee.

Being able to fly our family to Hawaii for only $80 (as opposed to $3000!) made our trip possible and left us plenty of money to spend on our actual vacation. Instead of scrimping and saving on this trip, we were able to stay in a luxury resort, enjoy amazing food and do all sorts of fun activities.

The trip coincided with our fifteenth wedding anniversary, my fortieth birthday, and our oldest son's ninth birthday. We couldn't have asked for a lovelier way to celebrate and it's made us realize that with a little bit of planning, we can make these kinds of special trips a more regular part of our family's lives."

As you can see from this family's story, this is something anyone with good credit and good sense can do. Not only did they get the vacation of their dreams, but they met their minimum spend by paying for things they were already paying for anyway.

What the Heck Is Minimum Spend?

Minimum spend is the **one-time** required amount to be spent on your credit card to receive the bonus miles offered. Some credit cards only require a first purchase. In other words, you buy a bottle of water with your new credit card and boom! You have enough miles to take a free flight to visit your family for the holidays. Most other cards require anywhere from $1,000 to $5,000 within a certain time frame, usually three to six months.

For example, a card might specify that if you spend $1,000 within the first three months of owning it, you then receive the bonus miles. Remember, it is a **one-time spend**. Once you've hit that minimum, you never have to do it again. And if you use the card to pay for as many of your regular bills/costs as possible, it should be fairly easy to reach your minimum spend within the required amount of time, and then you're ready to rock your travel.

Before we go any further, take a look at the miles/award chart to get a basic idea of how many FF miles you need for various flight options.

Average Miles Required for an Award Ticket
25,000 miles = 1 Domestic Economy Award Ticket
50,000 miles = 1 Domestic First Class Award Ticket
50,000 miles = 1 Intl. Economy Award Ticket
100,000 miles = 1 Intl. Business Class Award Ticket
125,000 miles = 1 Intl. First Class Award Ticket

Most airline co-branded credit cards offer at least a 25,000 FF mile bonus (which as you can see from the chart, equals one free flight in the U.S.). Many offer 30-40,000 FF mile bonuses and a few offer bonuses as high as 100,000 FF miles.

Continued on the next page ······▶

> To put that in perspective, you would have to fly from L.A. to N.Y. *five times* to earn 25,000 miles, or just one free flight. But getting one miles card will earn you anywhere from one free flight to four free flights without even setting foot on a plane.

Keep in mind that in addition to earning a ton of miles with sign-up bonuses, your new miles credit card will also reward you 1 FF mile for every dollar you spend on the card. Some cards even offer anywhere from two to five times the miles per dollar spent based on specific categories like groceries, travel, and dining. These miles can add up if you use your card strategically as Patrick and Emiliana did with their daily credit card.

For instance, think of all the bills and costs you pay in an average month. How many of them could be paid with a credit card and then *paid off completely* every month? Gas? Cable bill? Groceries? Rent? Cell Phone? Gym membership? In other words, pay for your usual stuff, and bingo, free flight from bonus miles plus *extra* FF miles for all the dollars you spent!

In addition, if you're currently using a debit card, why not switch those purchases to a credit card, and pay it off at the end of the month?

I spend around $1000 a month on food-related expenses for myself and my family. Using my airline co-branded credit card to pay groceries alone adds up to 12,000 miles per year. I've also got as many of my bills as possible being paid with my credit card, which I then *always* pay off completely at the end of the month.

Simply getting an airline miles credit card and using it solely for things you'd be spending money on anyway, you can meet the minimum spend, earn lots of airline miles, and have some amazing travel opportunities.

The irony is, despite the obvious benefits these cards can get you, most people probably wouldn't even bother to sign up for one.

Their reasons:

1. "I already have a miles card."

This drives me crazy. Simple math is all you need to realize that if you have a miles card and spend $25,000 USD on your card you will earn 25,000 FF miles, which is enough for one domestic award ticket. Don't get me wrong—25,000 miles is nothing to turn your nose up at. But credit card bonuses can earn you significantly more miles than simply using your current miles credit card.

If you were to apply for a few new mileage-earning credit cards and spend the same $25,000 USD on those cards instead (meeting their various minimum spends as you go), you'd earn 25,000 FF miles for spending $25,000, **plus an additional 120,000 FF miles from the sign-up bonuses** (assuming you got three cards in one year with 40k FF mile bonuses each) which would bring your total miles earned to 145,000 FF miles. That's enough for an International First Class flight to Europe or Asia *or* almost three International Coach flights.

2. "I wasn't planning to take a trip until *next* year."

That's not an excuse. That's an advantage. The more time you have to earn miles, the easier it will be to travel big for very little money. Most people who learn about the miles game regret that they didn't get into it sooner and start stockpiling miles so they would have tons of options whenever they are ready to travel.

3. "I don't want to fly American (United, British Airways, or insert your least favorite airline here)."

I understand. People sometimes have issues with certain airlines. Don't let that hold you back. You don't have to fly on the airline whose miles you earn.

Remember—airlines have alliances. For example, you can use American Airlines miles to fly First Class on Cathay Pacific. Cathay Pacific is consistently ranked as one of the best airlines in the world, with amazing First Class cabins. Don't pass up a huge sign-up bonus on an airline you might not otherwise fly because those miles could easily be used to fly a different airline.

And my personal favorite:

4. "No! I absolutely refuse to fly to Europe or anywhere amazing for free!"

In that case, put this book down immediately. Give it away to someone who actually wants to go somewhere.

Unless you've been abducted by aliens, there's no excuse for not taking advantage of such incredible opportunities.

It only takes a few minutes to apply and is totally worth the time. Having a few more credit cards is not that complicated and contrary to what many people believe, if you acquire more cards (and pay off their balances every month) it will raise your debt-to-credit ratio, which *raises* your credit score.

How Do I Choose?

You may be wondering what travel card is the right card for you. Choosing the right travel card or cards can seem tricky. There are so many cards out there and it's important to understand the value of the specific miles they are offering. Certain miles cards give you better value for your miles, depending on where in the world you're traveling to.

What's more, understanding the current details, benefits, and drawbacks of various cards, as well as knowing which cards are best for overall travel (airline and hotel) and also best for your personal travel interests is key. For this reason, I decided not to name specific cards in this book, but rather include them all on my website, where I can update them as changes occur.

On my website, I break down all the benefits and details of the best travel cards out there, including my personal favorites. There are also updates when crazy sign-up bonuses pop up that offer miles bonuses too huge to ignore. You can get all the Rock Star info at: rockyourtravel.com.

*****

Let's recap for a moment. Getting a miles card accomplishes several important steps in getting you to the dream destination of your choice.

- First, you earn a huge sign-up bonus. If it's not instantly enough to get you to your dream location, it's often 40-80% of the way there.
- Second, it allows you to earn miles on a daily basis, while using your card responsibly.

- Third, miles cards come with various travel perks that you can instantly take advantage of to improve your travel and save you money. A few examples are: Free Checked bags, Priority Check-in, yearly companion fares and flight miles bonuses.

CHAPTER 7

Becoming a Miles Millionaire

*"You are never too old to set another goal
or dream a new dream."*
—C.S. Lewis

I n this chapter, you will learn a powerful strategy for earning hundreds of thousands of FF miles very quickly. In fact, you can easily earn 200k (or more) FF miles in one afternoon by applying these techniques.

Now, I don't know how much money you make per hour, but I'm fairly certain if I asked you to spend one hour or less filling out a few forms and in return you'd earn two Business Class flights from the U.S. to Paris, France, or the dream location of your choice, you'd at least listen to what I had to say. Especially considering **each** Business Class flight would normally cost you anywhere from

$2000-$5000 USD. Multiply that by two and you've actually earned **$4000-$10,000 worth of airline travel in one hour.**

If you make that kind of money in an hour, then I should be reading *your* book. By the way, if you'd rather fly Economy, this translates to **four** round trip flights to Europe instead of two.

To break it down more simply, if you had 200,000 miles in your FF account that you wanted to redeem for award tickets and you wanted to fly from the U.S. to Europe or North Asia, you would be able to get:

1 Intercontinental round-trip First Class Award ticket
(125k miles each)

plus

1 Intercontinental round-trip Economy Award ticket
(50k miles each)

plus

1 Domestic round-trip Economy Award ticket
(25k miles each)

or

2 Intercontinental round-trip Business Class Award tickets
(100k miles each)

or

4 Intercontinental round-trip Economy Award tickets
(50k miles each)

If that's not crazy enough, if you have great credit, you can use this technique multiple times a year. Yes, it's truly ridiculous, but hey, this is America, where all things are possible.

Even better, this powerful technique doesn't even require you to fly a single mile to earn all these FF miles in the first place. Imagine the number of places you can visit and the adventures you could have with that many miles to burn.

Before I explain further, there are a few basics you need to know. If FF miles are your gateway to the world, credit card sign-up bonuses are the super-sonic jet plane that will get you there.

I must warn you, this strategy is not for everyone.

- It is **not** for people who are planning to buy a house or car soon. Using this technique properly should not put a large strain on your credit score; however, when looking to take out a large loan from a bank, they may consider multiple credit card applications as a red flag.
- It is **not** for people who don't have good credit. If you have poor credit, it will be more difficult for you to get approved for multiple cards.
- It is **not** for people who can't pay their credit cards off in *full* every month.
- It is **not** for people who can't handle having credit cards.
- It is **not** for people uncomfortable with getting multiple credit cards all at once or for people who have a secret addiction to the home shopping network.

This technique **is** for people who want to earn the most miles as quickly as possible, who have good credit, and are willing to use it responsibly to take advantage of amazing travel opportunities provided by airlines and banks. It is also the single most powerful technique for people who don't fly a lot to earn a ton of miles to allow them to travel the world at a fraction of the price it normally costs to fly.

What exactly is a Miles Millionaire anyway?

A Miles Millionaire is someone who has a million FF miles. The fastest way to become a Miles Millionaire is to leverage your good credit to get approved for multiple mileage-earning credit cards several times a year, enabling you to earn ridiculous amounts of FF miles.

Before you start:

Only choose credit cards that have a minimum spend that you can easily pay off.
This strategy does not save you money if you end up in debt. You must be able to completely pay off your credit cards every month for this to be a sound investment. If you don't have a lot of expenses, there are some cards where you receive the bonus miles/points immediately after your first purchase. That means you could simply go to the market and buy yourself a bottle of water for $1 and you would receive the bonus. A few examples of cards like this are the Bank of America Alaska Airlines Visa and the Barclays U.S. Airways MC. For more examples and credit card details, go to: rockyourtravel.com

Also, make sure to choose cards that have an annual fee that is manageable for you.

Find out your credit score.

The first thing you need to do is check your credit score. Your credit score is based on the assessment of three agencies: Experian, Transunion, and Equifax. Knowing what your credit score is will allow you to determine how many credit cards you can apply for at any given time. Annualcreditreport.com and myFICO.com are helpful websites in this regard.

Research which credit bureau the credit inquiry will come from.

Each credit card request is reflected in your credit score for two years. Sites like creditboards.com can give you a better idea of which credit cards use which credit agencies, so that when you apply for multiple cards, you can apply for ones which go through different agencies. This is important because if a bank sees too many inquiries (because you've applied for multiple cards that use a single agency for the credit check) you are more likely to be turned down.

A beginner example:

If your scores for all three agencies were 50 points over the required "good credit" score (700 or more) you could apply for one credit card from each agency every three months (4 times a year), for two years and get 24 new cards in a two-year span. Just make sure to check your credit with all three agencies before each new churn period.

At an average sign-up bonus of 40,000 FF miles per card, this modest churn method would earn you a **minimum of 480,000 FF miles per year.**

480,000 FF miles per year =

3 International First Class Flights
plus
1 International Business Class Flight

or

4 International Business Class Flights

plus

1 International Coach Flight

plus

1 U.S. Domestic Coach Flight

or

9 International Coach Flights

plus

1 U.S. Domestic Coach Flight

or

19 U.S. Domestic Coach Flights

Obviously there are other combinations, but this just shows you what's possible. Think of how many dream destinations you could fly to with that many miles. Plus, if you're a couple and you both do this churn, you can *double* the box above. The fact is, with credit card sign-up bonuses of 40,000, 50,000, 75,000, and even 100,000 miles available, it is often possible to do much better than this basic scenario.

Remember, credit inquiries are reflected in your credit score for two years. As stated earlier, websites like creditboards.com can give you an *idea* of which agency each card/bank uses, but knowing for sure which agency will review your credit app is not guaranteed.

As long as you pay on time and keep your balances below 50% of your credit limit, your credit score should remain stable or even improve. The credit agencies will lower your score by two to five points for each inquiry, but if you have a credit score of say, 750, even if you got hit for 5 points per card, if you signed up for four credit cards at once and they ALL were checked through one agency, you'd still have a good credit score of at least 730 and a giant cache of miles to travel with.

True mileage pros have got this down to a science and usually churn four to six cards every three months while maintaining good credit. If you want to take that step, make sure you do your research and watch your credit carefully.

I want to stress here, I am not a financial advisor, accountant, or money expert of any kind. I am simply presenting to you a common technique used by travel pros around the world to easily earn millions of FF miles. Credit rules and bank practices can change. Please make sure you do your research and understand your credit before you churn and as stated earlier, make sure you can afford to make the minimum spend, the annual fee, and your monthly bill before applying. Then you'll be ready to rock!

How does it feel to be a RST? And you didn't think it would be this easy, did you? It is.

Ahem, what if I apply for a credit card and don't get approved?

Usually when you apply for a credit card online you will receive an immediate reply about whether you've been approved or not. If your credit card application is denied, don't panic. Often these things are completely computerized and you just need to call the bank's customer service line and speak with an actual human.

There are many reasons you may have been denied that can be easily remedied when speaking to a live person. If you are freelance or run your own business, for example, speaking to a representative and explaining your income and work situation can be cause for immediate reconsideration and subsequent approval.

There are also questions you can ask and options you can offer in order to get the card of your choice. When it comes to reversing a credit card denial, talking to an actual person and being friendly and polite can make all the difference.

When you call, ask the person politely if they can tell you why you were denied. Being nice goes a long way in this process. It is useful to already know your credit score (hopefully it's a good one) and your approximate annual income. If either of those things are a factor, you can ask the customer service rep if they would be willing to grant you the card if you lowered the line of credit. It can be whatever their minimum is if that's what it takes.

If you are still having trouble, ask the rep what else there is you can do to get approved. Sometimes the red flag is something that can easily be taken care of or cleared up right then over the phone to pave the way for approval.

Also, if you already have a credit card with the bank in question, you can ask if they can lower the credit limit on your existing account and then approve you for the new card with a minimum line of credit. That way you still get the new card with the bonus miles and can prove to the bank that you are a reliable customer.

Carolyn Sykes is a professional harpist who's performed around the world and whose clients have included Maya Angelou, Bill Clinton, and Queen Nor of Jordon. She teaches harp at her own music studio, Pacific Harps (www.pacificharps.com) and also provides music for special events through her company, Music for Events (www.music-for-events.com).

However, running a successful business rather than getting a payroll check can sometimes confuse credit card companies, causing them to reject an application from someone clearly qualified to receive it.

Here's how Carolyn changed her credit card status from "declined" to "approved" in one phone call.

Carolyn Sykes

"Last year Algis told me about a great deal on a Chase Miles Card: If I applied for their card I would get 50k Frequent Flyer miles for applying and then another 50k Frequent Flyer miles over the next few months for using the card. So I applied immediately. That's a Business Class ticket to Europe! I got my letter from them a week later saying that I had been declined. I was very disappointed.

Algis suggested that I call them back and see what I could negotiate. Since the card was being issued by Chase, and I already had a different Chase card with a high credit limit, Algis suggested that I ask Chase if I could lower my limit on my current card to allow me to get the new miles card.

So I called Chase and talked to a representative, and she thought that the idea would work. I didn't need to speak to a supervisor and it didn't take very long. In a week I had my card. And I now have 120k FF miles!"

PART 3
Flying Like a Rock Star

CHAPTER 8
Booking Flights

*"I am not an Athenian or a Greek,
I am a citizen of the world."*
—Socrates

Here are some general guidelines to aid you in acquiring the best deals with the least amount of time and hassle. Keep in mind there are always exceptions, so please use this as a guide, not a gospel.

Booking Your Flight

The best (cheapest) days to FLY are usually: Tuesday, Wednesday, and Saturday.

The best (cheapest) days to BUY U.S. domestic flights tend to be: from Tuesday through Thursday.

The best seasons for deals: Shoulder season/Off-season.
Surprise, surprise, if you choose to go somewhere when others aren't there, the demand for both flights and hotels will be less and you'll find much lower prices for both.

For example, if you're flying from L.A. to Australia, it's going to be most expensive in Dec./Jan. because although that is winter in the U.S., it's summer in Australia—hence the most popular time to visit Oz. It all depends on why you are visiting a place and what you want to get out of it. If you don't mind a bit of rain, for instance, Paris in March will be significantly cheaper than Paris in June, July, and August.

Getting the best seats: When you are booking your flight online, after you've chosen your dates and exact flights, you will be given an opportunity to select your seats from a seat map. Look and see what seats are available on your airline's website. But *before* you choose, open another tab in your browser and go to **seatguru. com** to view a seat map of your plane and see how the available seats rate, so you can make an informed decision instead of just guessing or simply allowing the airline to choose your seat. If you let the airlines pick for you, chances are you'll end up sitting in the very back, or next to a bathroom, and/or most likely in a middle seat with two new friends on either side of you… generally, not the best way to start a vacation.

Booking via a Consolidator (Expedia, Hotline, etc.) vs. booking on an airline (United Airlines, American Airlines, etc.) website.

If your only goal is to find the cheapest tickets, then consolidators can be a good way to go, as they will search multiple airlines all in one place. I usually start my search for flights with **Kayak.com** and/or **Hipmunk.com** (two of my favorite search engines). This gives me an idea of how much a particular flight will cost on a variety of airlines.

Finding the lowest price is not the only consideration when buying tickets. Earning FF miles is a huge part of my travel strategy. Whenever possible, I choose flights that earn miles in my "main" FF program, or a program that I want miles in, rather than fly a discount airline whose miles I have no interest in (Spirit, Frontier, etc.).

After finding a flight I want, I go to that airline's website to book the flight directly. You don't have to do this; you can book through the consolidator. However, if something goes wrong with your ticket (flight delay, cancellation, etc.) you will be stuck dealing with Expedia or whatever consolidator you used, instead of dealing with the airline directly, and often, the consolidator will not notify you of cancellations or changes like the airlines would.

Booking Free Flights (Redeeming Miles for Flight Awards)

Now that you'll be earning heaps of miles using the information in the previous chapters, let's discuss the best ways to use those miles. The strategies below will help you decide how to spend your miles appropriately and achieve your travel goals.

The Value of Frequent Flyer Miles: The value of FF miles varies based on how you redeem them. For example, if you redeem 25,000 FF miles for a domestic Economy Class award flight that would normally cost $350 USD to purchase, then you are essentially getting 1.4 cents of value per FF mile.

An example of a better value would be choosing to redeem your FF miles for an International Business Class ticket. You could use 100,000 FF miles for an International Business Class flight award that would normally cost $5,000 USD and essentially receive 5 cents of value per FF mile. When possible, I strongly suggest using miles primarily for overseas travel, preferably in Business Class.

When airfares are low, most Frequent Flyers opt to buy the tickets instead of using miles to get them. This strategy saves their miles for a more expensive trip or for when fares go up, therefore providing more value. However, if you don't have the cash to spare and you do have the miles to burn, by all means use your miles and get the free trip. FF miles should help you save money on travel and get you where you want to go, so use them in ways that work for you.

Use Your Miles for a Trip You Couldn't Otherwise Afford: With FF miles, you can easily earn enough miles to fly Economy to wherever you want to go. However, I would encourage you to use your miles to the fullest and consider flying Business Class or First Class on your miles. This is one of the areas where Frequent Flyer travel really shines. It enables you to take dream trips and travel in a manner in which you would not otherwise be able to afford.

Most people are not comfortable spending $3,000-$6,000 USD to fly Business Class to their dream destination, but by using Frequent Flyer miles that can be earned quickly and easily from Mileage Credit Card Bonuses, your dream trip to Machu Pichu in Peru, the beautiful beaches of the Virgin Islands, the Colosseum in Rome, or wherever you've been wanting to go, can become a reality.

When **You Fly Affects How Easy it is to Get Award Seats:** Flying mid-week gives you the best chance to score award tickets, as does having some flexibility in your schedule and traveling in the off-season or shoulder-season, whereas getting an award flight on Thanksgiving weekend when *everyone* in the States is traveling is going to be tough.

Taxes, Fees and Fuel Surcharges:
Even with a "free" award ticket, you will still be required to pay airport and government fees. They are usually quite low. For example: It only costs $52.50 in fees to fly roundtrip on American Airlines from Los Angeles to Tokyo. However, many foreign carriers also charge a "Fuel Surcharge." As a general rule, U.S. carriers do not. One exception to the rule is if you are redeeming an American Airlines award for a Brittish Airways flight.

Keep Your Eyes Open for Discounted Award Flights:
I recently booked a Business Class flight from San Francisco to Tokyo on Japan Airlines (JAL) with American Airlines miles (remember they are OneWorld Partners) for 50,000 miles round-trip instead of the normal 100,000 miles for the same flight. I'll take 50% off anytime!

Don't Assume Awards Aren't Available Because You Can't See Them Online.
Remember when we talked about airlines belonging to alliances and how you could use American Airlines miles to take a flight to Australia on Qantas, one of American Airlines' OneWorld partners? Well, it's important to note that when you go on the American Airlines website and look for award availability using their search engine, it won't show you *all* its partner awards. It will only show you awards available on American Airlines, airberlin, Alaska Airlines, British Airways, Finnair, Hawaiian Airlines, and Qantas. That means if you want to use American Airlines

FF miles to book and fly one of their other OneWorld partners (Cathay Pacific, Iberia, Japan Airlines, LAN, Royal Jordinian, or S7 Airlines) you will have to call American Airlines to do so.

Also, you can find out when there are awards available on American Airlines' Alliance Partners by going on BritishAirways.com or Qantas.com to search for award availability. Those airline websites show much more accurate availability of OneWorld airline awards. But even *they* don't show all the possibilities.

Regardless, remember not to just give up if you do a search on your airline's website and an award does not come up. Make sure and call the airline to see if they have any awards available on one of their partner airlines.

Although United Airlines is better about showing award availability for their various partners on its website, you can use the technique of looking on Air Canada's or ANA's websites if you want to do a more thorough search before calling United to book your award flight and/or ask about availability.

Strategies for Dealing With Airline Booking Agents:
Always remember you have some control. If you get an agent who is not helpful or unwilling to check various routings or just seems like they'd rather be anywhere else but talking on the phone with you, simply hang up and call back. You will get another agent, hopefully with a better disposition, and you won't have wasted a bunch of your time.

How Far in Advance Should You Book an Award Flight?
It really helps to plan ahead. Award seats are made available as far as 330 days in advance. While it is possible to book them then, the airlines also hold back some award seats and only make them available later. It is good to check six months out and also very close to the date you'd like to travel. Although not everyone can do this,

if you have a lot of flexibility like I do, you will also often be able to score tickets three days to a week or two before your flight.

Keep in mind, award seats are not always available on the exact dates you want, so being flexible with your dates and/or routing can really help secure the seats you want.

Consider Alternate Routing and/or a Nearby Location.

If your goal is to fly from Dallas to Paris, but no award tickets are available on the dates you'd like to travel, you could instead fly from Dallas to Madrid on an award ticket (assuming it's available) and then purchase an inexpensive ticket from Madrid to Paris.

Alternatively, if there are no non-stops from Dallas to Paris, you may find that a routing that goes from Dallas to Philadelphia to Paris has award space available. While slightly less convenient, it still allows you to use your award and receive tremendous value from your miles.

What if You Really, Really, NEED that Flight on a specific Date?

Use an "Anytime" award. These awards usually cost twice the amount of FF miles a "Saver" award costs, but they will be available at times (think heavy travel days, blackout days, etc.) when "Saver" awards are hard to come by.

What if You're Trying to Book Award Seats for a Family?

One option is to get as many award seats as possible and just buy the rest of the tickets. Make sure the person who travels the most flies on the *purchased* ticket so they can earn or maintain Elite Status with the airline.

Having just one family member with Elite Status can make a big difference for everyone. For instance, if you're on your way to

Europe with the family and only you have Elite Status, it doesn't mean that the rest of the family has to stand in the normal check-in and security lines. In fact, they get to go with you to the Elite Check-in counter, the much shorter Elite Security line, and even board the plane early. As long as you are all booked on the same record number, many of your Elite Status benefits will be extended to the rest of the family when traveling together.

Another option to use when there simply aren't enough award seats on one flight for the whole family is to split up and take separate flights, sometimes even on different days. While less convenient, this is still a viable option if your goal in the miles game is to spend as little as possible. This may sound strange, but I would argue that the time you spend sitting on the plane is the least valuable family time during your trip. Again, this is a "choose your own adventure" game, just like life.

What If There Are No Economy Awards Available?

Shame on you for even thinking of flying in Economy. What sort of self-respecting RST would fly in economy? I kid. I joke. Seriously, there are usually more award seats available in Business and/or First Class because the Economy awards go first. Why? Because they're cheaper. Why not step up and enjoy the luxury of Business or First Class? As I stated earlier, this is where the true value of FF miles really presents itself. If you have the miles, why not use them and enjoy all the perks of flying in the front of the plane. The only drawback is you may never want to go back to flying in Economy.

As a Last Resort:

You can book flights using Starwood hotel points also. In this case you call Starwood and they will buy the flight from the airline. You will usually get the flight you want on the date you want and you will earn FF miles because the flight will count as a paid flight, not an award redemption. However, this is generally not the best value for Starwood Starpoints.

CHAPTER 9

Visiting Multiple Cities for the Price of One Award

Stopovers, Open-Jaws, and Free One-Ways

"Life itself is the proper binge."
—Julia Child

L earning about these three routing rules will allow you to get the maximum value out of the FF Award Tickets you book. In this section, I will define how stopovers, open-jaws, and free one-ways work and how you can use them to construct amazing FF Award trips.

Stopovers

A stopover is a stop in your itinerary that is more than 24 hours in a city other than your destination city. It can be for as long as you want (one day, one week, one month, etc.), so long as your entire itinerary is completed within one year. So, although unlikely, you could have an 11-month stopover on your way to your destination city. This is a very nice routing rule as you can visit two countries for the price of one award. That adds some serious value.

I'm going to use Alaska Airlines for this example. If you book an award ticket using Alaska Airlines FF miles to fly to Tokyo, then you can fly Alaska's partner airline, Cathay Pacific (one of the best, and one of my personal favorite airlines, in the sky). If you're unclear on how this works, review partners and alliances in Chapter 5.

Cathay Pacific has a hub in Hong Kong and they route their flights to Asia via Hong Kong. Since Alaska Airlines allows a stopover, you can stop in Hong Kong for as long as you want before continuing to Tokyo.

On Alaska, a stopover is only allowed in one direction, so you'd have to decide whether you'd prefer to do this on the outbound or on the return. Different airlines have different routing rules. Some allow stopovers in each direction (United Airlines, for example), while some only allow a stopover in one direction (Alaska Airlines).

Open-Jaws

An open-jaw is when you A.) fly into one city and then fly back from a different city, or B.) fly from one city and then fly back to a different city.

Here are a few examples:

San Francisco to Paris outbound followed by London to San Francisco return. How you get from Paris to London is up to you and is not included in the fare of an open-jaw, regardless if it is an open-jaw award ticket or an open-jaw paid ticket. This is a great ticket to get if you want to visit two locations in one trip without having to backtrack to the first location. Fly to Paris, enjoy your time there then take the Chunnel to London and continue your vacation until you return home from London.

The other option with an open-jaw is to have your return flight take you to another city. Fly from Los Angeles to Paris then on the return fly Paris to San Francisco. Again, you will be responsible for getting from San Francisco to Los Angeles later if you need to do so.

A great way to take advantage of an open-jaw is when you are visiting a region with multiple countries that you want to see, or a large country which you want to traverse, without the added time of backtracking.

Free One-Ways

Adding a free one-way award is an advanced use of a stopover, which involves adding a one-way segment to the end of your itinerary. This one-way segment would be to another city in the country you are originating from and returning to. I will use the U.S. as an example.

If you live in New York and are traveling to Europe and your itinerary is New York to London then London to New York, you could add on a New York to San Francisco segment at the end of your return flight at no extra cost. Keep in mind that the free-one way (New York to San Francisco) could happen up to 11 months later than your initial round-trip.

PART 4
Travel Better

CHAPTER 10
Elite Status

"A fool wanders, a wise man travels."
—Thomas Fuller

'm running late. I hop out of the cab, gather my bags, and head to departures and check-in. It's bedlam in there. There are people everywhere, kids lying on the floor, a family of 12 repacking their luggage, a couple bickering way too loud, bored teenagers draped over their suitcases eating candy bars next to a yappy dog barking from inside what he clearly knows is a cat carrier.

The line to check in is easily more than 100 people. I start to panic, but just then, I remember my Elite Status. I casually walk over to the Elite Check-in line… where there is no line. In fact, there are three agents just waiting there for someone, anyone, to help.

So while the rest of the uninformed masses glare at me, I stroll to the front desk, where the agents welcome me, check me in, and process my baggage quickly and painlessly. They then inform me that my checked bag (a rarity for me) will be free due to my Elite Status.

They point me in the direction of the Elite Security line, so I can have a much swifter and smoother transition from the check-in area to the gates. I breathe a sigh of relief as I realize I definitely won't be late for my flight.

What is Elite Status?

Elite Status is like having a VIP card from an individual airline (and that airline's alliances) that rewards you with a multitude of perks not offered to the "average flyer." There are benefits ranging from being upgraded to First or Business Class, to having your baggage fees waived. Below is a list of some of the great benefits Elite Status offers.

Shorter Security Lines

Elite Status allows you to use the Elite Security line. Not only is this special line usually much shorter, but also, since most people in this line are experienced travelers, the line moves faster. Yes, this means less time standing in line to get to your gate. Like most people, I don't exactly savor standing in lines. So I really love this benefit.

Shorter Check-In Lines

There is a separate dedicated check-in line for Elites and First/ Business Class flyers. Once you've attained Elite Status (even if you are flying Coach), you can still use the Elite line to check-in and check your bags. This can really be a time saver when you're running late.

Early Boarding

Early boarding gets you on the plane before people who don't have Elite Status. What this means is even when you are flying Coach, you still get on the plane before most coach passengers and can therefore easily find overhead space for your bags. This translates to more legroom.

Extra Frequent Flyer Miles Earned

As you've already learned in the Earning Miles section of the book, when you have Elite Status, you earn bonus Frequent Flyer miles. This means you'll rack up more free flights even faster. The chart on p. 45-6 shows how many bonus miles you earn with various airlines depending on your level of Elite Status. At the top level of Elite Status you'll be earning a 100% bonus on the miles you fly, which means you'll be earning free flights twice as fast as a non-Elite flyer.

Access to Airport Lounges

Certain levels of Elite Status can grant you complimentary access to airport lounges around the world. If you have Elite Status with an American carrier, you won't have free access to domestic lounges (within the U.S.). But hey, now that you're traveling the world, you'll have plenty of opportunities to enjoy lounges in other countries. An interesting side-note, however—if you have certain levels of Elite Status with a *non-US airline*, then you *can* get free access to U.S. lounges. Ironic, but true!

In addition, with the right level of Elite Status, you'll have access to these airport lounges even when traveling in Coach! If you're wondering what the heck an airport lounge is, don't worry. You'll learn all about airport lounges in the next chapter and once you do, you'll understand what a fantastic perk this really is.

Waived Checked Baggage Fees

Now that the airlines are charging for checking your bag, it's nice to know that having Elite Status can get you out of that. This can be a very good savings if the whole family is traveling. If you are all on the same record number and even if only one person has Elite Status, up to four people can check a bag for free. Considering that airlines now charge as much as $25 for the first bag (per person), for a family of four that becomes a savings of $100 per flight, each way. That's a $200 savings for a round-trip flight.

Ability to Receive Free Upgrades to First or Business Class

Flying First Class, without paying for First Class, never gets old and the best way to get those kind of upgrades is by having Elite Status. Every airline has a slightly different system so it's best to go to their website and read about their rules and regulations regarding Elite member upgrades.

A few things to keep in mind about upgrades:

1. The higher your status, the better your chance of receiving upgrades and the more upgrades you will receive. For example, at the top tier of American Airlines Elite Status (Executive Platinum), you are entitled to unlimited domestic upgrades based on availability. That means, pay for Coach, fly First Class (when First Class seats are available).

On the mid-level and entry-level tiers of American Airlines Elite Status (Platinum and Gold, respectively) you earn 500-mile upgrade vouchers and must have enough of them to cover the distance of the segment you wish to upgrade. This means the more you fly, the more upgrades you can earn and then choose to apply to certain flights. You will get them based on availability and priority. Higher levels of Elite Status have upgrade priority.

2. Some fare classes are not eligible for upgrades. That means if you bought the cheapest ticket available, you may not be able to upgrade it. I'd recommend checking your airline's policy to see what fare classes are eligible for upgrades before purchasing tickets.

Better Customer Service

Earning Elite Status is a sign of your loyalty to a specific airline. An airline wants to keep its best customers happy so they go the extra mile for passengers with Elite Status. This includes having dedicated phone numbers with much shorter wait times for Elites based on your level. Also, many fees such as change fees and ticketing service charges are waived for top-level Elites. In general, you will be treated better by the airlines if you have Elite Status.

So How the Heck Do I Get Elite Status?

Elite Status is earned by flying a set amount of miles on a given airline. Entry-level Elite Status usually starts at 25k miles **flown** (that means your butt actually in the seat), but this varies slightly by airline. However, there are also some great RST shortcuts to earning Elite Status.

- **Elite Status Challenges**
- **Elite Status Matches**
- **Buying Elite Status**

Instead of taking multiple flights to earn Elite Status, these secret shortcuts can earn you Elite Status instantly. I told you you'd get your money's worth!

Elite Status Challenges

Two airlines that offer Elite Status Challenges are American Airlines and U.S. Airways.

The American Airlines Gold or Platinum Elite Status Challenge

This challenge can help you earn Elite Status in one-fifth the time it would normally take.

The American Airlines Elite Status Challenge is a very fast and easy way to qualify for Elite Status. However, you won't find any of this information on their website. You just have to magically know about it, and *voila!* Now you do.

This challenge basically entails flying enough to earn 5,000 Elite-Qualifying Points (instead of the usual 25,000 Elite-Qualifying Miles) for Gold Status or flying enough to earn 10,000 Elite-Qualifying Points (instead of the usual 50,000 Elite-Qualifying Miles) for Platinum Status, within a *three-month* timeframe.

You will be given the choice of starting on the 1st or the 16th of the month. The good news is, you can backdate when you start the challenge, so if you are going to take a flight on the 8th of January and it's the 5th of January when you call customer service, ask them to start your challenge from the 1st of January even though that has already passed.

Once you've registered for the Gold or Platinum Challenge, you will most likely receive an email from American Airlines telling you the basic rules. It will probably give you some information such as:

You must fly on American Airlines, American Eagle, or AmericanConnection to earn AA points that count towards the challenge.

Challenges are based on points (not miles) so fares with high point values earn you Elite Status faster. Deep discount fares are only worth half a point per mile that the regular discount fares are worth. With a regular discount fare, you can earn Platinum Status after flying 10,000 Elite-Qualifying Points (If you've registered for the Gold Challenge, you will only need to earn 5,000 EQPs). If you choose premium fares (aka Business/First Class) you'll earn 1.5 points per mile and you can meet the challenge even faster.

When you book a flight, there are booking codes that will tell you how many Elite-Qualifying points you will earn per mile based on their letter.

For example: An American Airlines ticket that's booked using one of these code letters (A F P D I J R B C Y) is worth 1.5 points per mile.
AA tickets booked with the codes (H K L M V W) earn 1 point per mile.
AA tickets booked with codes (G N Q S O) earn a half a point per mile.

If you book your flight on AA.com, the Flight Summary Screen will display the booking code in the same column as the cabin booked. Or you can ask your booking agent/travel agent when booking through them.

To register for this challenge, you need to call American Airlines customer service (800-882-8880) and *ask* to start the challenge. It will cost you $120 for the Gold Status Challenge and $240 for the Platinum Status Challenge. This fee is non-refundable. You pay up front and will not get your money back if you don't complete the challenge. American Airlines gives you 90 days to fly the required miles.

A few more things to keep in mind: You will not be able to re-qualify and maintain Elite Status using an Elite Status Challenge the following year, you will have to qualify by flying the normal amount of miles necessary to maintain Status.

When you start your challenge is important. If you start your challenge *before* June 16th, your Elite Status will last for the remainder of that year and through the first two months of the following year. For example, if you start on January 1, 2013, and then complete it within three months, your status will last until the end of February 2014 (giving you up to 14 months worth of status). However, if you start your challenge *on or after* June 16th, your status will last for the remainder of that year, the entire following year and the first two months of the year after—nearly 20 months worth of status.

For example, if you start on June 16th, 2013, and complete your challenge within three months, your status will last all the way until the end of February 2015. So, if you have the option, I'd recommend starting after June 16th.

U.S. Airways Elite Status Challenge

Okay, if one-fifth the time isn't fast enough for you, you can undertake the U.S. Airways Trial Preferred Program and earn status instantly.

Select and purchase the level of Preferred status that you want. Silver—$200, Gold—$400, Platinum—$600. You will receive that level of status **immediately** so you can see how you like it.

Unlike the American Airlines Status Challenge, US Airways counts miles flown, rather than points. You will receive 90 days to complete the challenge by flying a set amount of miles on flights operated by U.S. Airways. The amount of miles varies by level of status that you are seeking. Here's the list:

- Silver: Fly 7,500 miles.
- Gold: Fly 15,000 miles.
- Platinum: Fly 22,500 miles.
- Chairman's: Fly 30,000 miles.

A few important things to keep in mind:

If you purchase Silver Status for $200, but end up flying 15,000 miles during the 90-day challenge period, you will end up receiving Gold Status. Pretty cool, right? Did you see that? I just saved you $200 bucks ($400 if you fly 22,500 miles and score Platinum Status for only $200 bucks).

Once you meet the flying requirement, you will keep whatever level of status you qualified for until the end of February of the following year. For example, if you qualify for Gold on March 19, 2012, you will have Gold Status until February 28, 2013.

Elite Status Matches

Alaska Airlines will match whatever airline status you have on another airline, up to their (Alaska's) mid-tier, MVP-Gold. All you have to do is contact them and then email or fax a current copy of your member card or mileage statement (from the airline program you already have status with!) and include your Alaska Airlines Mileage Plan account #. The status will be valid through the end of the year. Of course, you could certainly fly enough to re-qualify and earn it for the subsequent year.

Elite Status Match Challenges

If you already have Elite Status with one airline but decide you'd like to switch your loyalty to a different airline in a competing Alliance, you can contact the airline you are interested in and find out if they offer an Elite Status Match Challenge.

If they do, they will temporarily grant you Elite Status, give you 90 days to complete their "challenge" and fly a set amount of miles. If you complete the challenge, they will award you status for the balance of their program's year so you can enjoy the benefits of your new airline instead.

Buying Elite Status

If you have more money than time and just want instant Elite Status, U.S. Airways is willing to oblige you. They will sell you Elite Status even if you've never flown with them at all!

- Their top Status, Chairman's Preferred, costs $3,999.
- Their high mid-level, Platinum, is $2,999.
- Their low mid-level, Gold, is $2,499.
- Their entry level, Silver, is $1,499.

While this is decidedly not a good deal for the casual traveler, it may be something to look into if you love shortcuts, and can't live without Elite Status.

CHAPTER 11
Airline Lounges

*"I never travel without my diary.
One should always have something sensational
to read in the train."*
—Oscar Wilde

'm reclining in a massage chair. I've been here for 30 minutes and I'll be here for 30 more. I'm in my own little world. Relaxing. I've already enjoyed two rounds of dim sum and a cold beer. My girlfriend is in a separate cubicle also relaxing in a massage chair. Did I mention we are at the *airport*?

I know it sounds crazy, but I love going to the airport early. Our flight boards in about an hour. We are not stressed. We are savoring being in the Sakura Lounge. It's an exclusive airport lounge in Tokyo, and since we used miles to fly Business Class, we have free access to it and the **free** amenities within: food, beer, liquor, Internet, massage chairs, and plenty of peace and quiet.

Sakura Lounge, Haneda Airport, Tokyo, Japan

Airport Lounges are your gateway to a secret world of comfortable spacious chairs, free beverages (yes this often includes alcohol), and tasty complimentary (another word for free) snacks that will guarantee you will never want to go back to the cattle call areas where the uninformed masses congregate.

You may be surprised to find that almost every airline has a lounge, just not in every airport. Simply ask someone at the ticket counter where their airline lounge is and cruise over there.

When it comes to accessing Airline Lounges, you have a number of options:

Traveling on an International First or Business Class Ticket – You get complimentary access on the day of your flight. This includes paid and award tickets. So that's another reason to book a First/Business Class award.

Elite Status – Those who have mid-level or above Elite Status are generally granted access to their airline's club lounges and often alliance lounges as well, even on an Economy Class ticket, so long as they are flying internationally. Rules can vary. Check your preferred airline for their specific airline lounge policies.

Traveling with Someone Who Has a Membership – Members of American Airlines, Delta, United Airlines, and/or U.S. Airways are allowed to bring two guests or their immediate family into the lounge with them.

One-Day Passes – These can be purchased at the airport lounge for $50 USD.

Yearly Memberships – Yearly memberships generally cost around $500 (although they often run specials). You may feel like you don't want to pay this extra fee, but an airport lounge can be the difference between an awful layover with an extremely uncomfortable wait in the main airport or a chance to relax, catch up on some e-mail (using the free Wi-Fi or PCs), watch TV, grab a shower (yes many really do have showers), eat some snacks, have some drinks and get some business done if necessary. Some lounges, like Heathrow's British Airways First, even have spas with masseuses!

Priority Pass Membership – Similar to buying a yearly club membership, except Priority Pass gives you access to more than 600 lounges worldwide that span various airlines (and even some independent lounges) instead of just from one airline. For example, at Los Angeles International Airport, you would have access to any of the following lounges: U.S. Airways Club, Air Canada Maple Leaf Lounge, Air France Business Class Lounge, United Club, Alaska Airlines Board Room, Relax Lounge, and/or the Skyteam KAL Business Class Lounge. Priority Pass has a few levels of membership, starting at $99 per year with a $27 per visit fee all the way up to $399 per year for a Prestige membership where all visits are included free. Some AMEX cards even give you Priority Pass membership free as one of their benefits. Currently the Platinum AMEX, the Morgan Stanley Smith Barney Platinum AMEX, the Ritz-Carlton AMEX, and the Mercedes-Benz Platinum AMEX all provide this benefit.

Having the Right Credit Card – Having the right credit card will give you access to Airline Lounges. In addition to the AMEX cards listed above, American, Delta, and United all have at least one co-branded credit card that will entail the bearer to free lounge access. These cards include the Citi AAdvantage World

Elite Mastercard, Delta Reserve AMEX, and the Chase United MileagePlus Club Card.

If you want to know more about the best travel credit cards and their individual perks/drawbacks, go to my website at: rockyourtravel.com for a detailed breakdown before deciding what card is right for you.

Not All Lounges Are Created Equal

Yes, it's true. Some lounges are far nicer than others. However, when it comes to International Lounges, even the average ones usually have complimentary drinks (water, juice, soda, beer, coffee drinks, liquor) and snacks ranging from bags of chips, to cookies, to apples, etc., and even small prepared finger sandwiches. They also include their own fancy bathrooms, comfortable club chairs, sofas, Wi-Fi, and are much quieter than the rest of the airport.

The best lounges, Heathrow British Airways First Class Lounge, for example, have full bars, nice wine selections, sit-down restaurants with wait staff, free internet, a salon with massages, showers, complimentary haircuts and possibly other perks I have yet to discover. Remember all of the above is *free*!

Keep in mind, international lounges like Heathrow have way more perks than domestic ones. Some domestic lounges charge for food and drinks, just like the rest of the airport.

Make sure you ask what amenities the lounge offers and also check which airports they have locations in so if you choose a yearly membership, it can be in places you are most likely to frequent.

Now you know the secret and you can start your vacation even before your flight leaves.

Steven Lanza
Hermosa Beach, California

"*I travel a lot and had been in airline lounges before, but never with my family. Usually my wife and I would plan to be at the airport with our kids as late as possible before taking a flight. However, our most recent trip was a long-awaited family vacation to the Cayman Islands and we decided to get to the airport with plenty of time to spare. We didn't want to take any chances on missing our flight, so we ended up past security and waiting for our plane hours before the scheduled flight.*

A while back, Algis had suggested I take the whole family in the lounge on our next trip, but I was hesitant. My experience in lounges before was that they were quiet and peaceful and the thought of bringing my kids into a lounge when they were all amped up for a trip and then keeping them calm for two hours until our plane left sounded exhausting, to say the least. But with all that time to spare at the airport, we thought we'd give it a try. It turned out to be the best thing we could've done before our flight.

We were in the American Airlines International Lounge at LAX, which is pretty spacious, and because we were there during the day, the Lounge was very empty. We saw that they had a soundproof (or seemingly so) kids' room enclosed on one side in glass and decided to hang out in there. Our kids are older, eight and thirteen years., but this room was set up for kids and families of all ages. We could have hung out in any of the other areas of the lounge (there are areas with giant windows, a smaller area with sports TV, etc.) but this room had everything a family could want while waiting. Low tables to do puzzles and games, computers and Internet access for older kids, wood blocks and balls for toddlers, etc. Plus it had a bench seat that went all the way around the room, so my wife and I could stretch out or even lie down if we wanted.

Next to the family room, there was a bar and restaurant. A waitress came in and took our order, and then brought all the food back into our area. It was great. We had pizza and drinks, the kids were occupied, and when it was time to fly, we all felt relaxed and rested rather than stressed and tired.

Whether you're alone and looking for peace and quiet, or with your family, airport lounges are definitely the way to go."

CHAPTER 12

Some Expert Advice

"You only live once, but if you do it right, once is enough."
—Mae West

Travel is many things to many people. A respite from your daily routine; an opportunity to reinvent yourself; an adventure into the unknown; a chance to see, taste, and experience another culture; an awakening; a gentle push to expand your mind and so much more.

Travel forces you to live in the moment. It makes the most jaded feel young. It is the antidote to being stuck in a rut. While many people may view travel as a luxury, I believe it is vital.

One of the main reasons for writing this book was to remove the belief that you can't afford to travel by showing you ways to make travel inexpensive. I hope I've accomplished that.

However, there are many other areas of travel in which a little knowledge can enhance your entire experience and in some cases, even quell travel concerns you may have. For this reason, I've asked a number of my friends (all experts in their fields) to offer their advice on how to make your trip the best it can be.

What to Pack When Traveling Expert Advice from Sean Bonner

Seanbonner.com

It's rather difficult to explain what Sean Bonner does exactly. It's kind of a secret, in fact. A mystery, actually. To be honest, we don't like to talk about it much. But on occasion, he is willing to share his super- human traveling expertise. This is one of those occasions.

Sean Bonner

Few things can ruin a trip like losing your bags. Or having things stolen from your bags. Or worrying about things getting stolen from your bags. Or standing around at baggage claim waiting forever stressing because your bag hasn't shown up yet and everyone else already has their bag and why isn't your bag here yet and, crap, your bag probably got lost. Trust me on this, the most important travel tip I could ever bestow is this: only suckers check bags. All carry-on all the time is the only way to go. Think that's crazy? People who check bags are crazy! Here's some tips to help you never have to check a bag again.

The most important thing to add to your travel kit: An elastic clothesline with hooks that you can hang in a hotel bathroom to let clothes dry. 30 minutes of washing clothes in a bathroom sink beats the crap out of lugging a giant suitcase all over the world.

Only pack things you know you will use on your trip. You don't need a full wardrobe of options, you know where you are going and what you'll be doing there, so pack with that in mind. Don't bring anything "just in case."

If you need something you didn't bring, chances are you can buy it when you get there. If you have to choose between bringing something you might not use, or not bringing something you may need, err on the side of not bringing it.

Never put a jacket in your suitcase, wear it or carry with you and throw it into the overhead compartment on the plane.

Put everything you plan to take on your bed before packing it so you can see everything at once. What's missing? What is redundant?

Roll clothes, don't fold. Pack the biggest stuff first, then use the smaller stuff to fill the gaps.

Learn from your mistakes. If after your trip you have things in your suitcase that you never touched, make sure not to bring them next time.

Tripit
Sean Bonner

I'm standing in the hotel lobby of the Granbell Hotel in Shibuya chatting with the clerk. I've just checked out and have a ticket on the NE'X train to Narita Airport in an hour and a flight back to Los Angeles shortly thereafter.

Then I get a text message from TripIt Pro, telling me that my flight has been cancelled. Luckily, I'm able to call the airline from the hotel and get booked on a new flight in a matter of minutes and continue on my way to the airport as if nothing happened.

Two hours later, I get an email notification from the airline that my original flight has been cancelled. Out of curiosity I take a look, and every flight back for the next two days is now sold out. If it wasn't for that notification from TripIt, I'd have been stranded for days.

Without question, the best travel-related money I spend every year is on TripIt Pro. On its own, TripIt is a handy organizational tool—keeping all of your travel plans in one place, tracking your miles and points, and letting you know which of your friends will be crossing your global path—but all it takes is one situation like what I just went through in Tokyo to know the price of the Pro account is totally worth it.

Staying Healthy While Traveling
Dr. Brett White

http://www.ohsu.edu/xd/health/services/providers/whiteb.cfm

Brett White, M.D. is an Associate Professor and the Medical Director of the Gabriel Park Family Health Center at the Oregon Health & Science University (OHSU) in Portland, Oregon. He is also the Associate Program Director of the OHSU Family Medicine Residency as well as the Director of Student Development in the OHSU School of Medicine.

Dr. White helped to develop an international travel clinic based at the Gabriel Park Family Health Center where resident physicians learn about travel health. He has more than 30 publications, has given presentations nationally and internationally and has also been voted a "Portland Top Doctor."

He also loves camping, playing electric guitar, eating delicious Mexican food, and answering travel questions posed by yours truly. Below are some of my questions and Dr. White's answers on how to stay healthy and happy while traveling.

An interview with Dr. Brett White
What are the best U.S. resources for health and travel?

The most important website for travelers to explore before going abroad is the Center for Disease Control (CDC) Traveler's Health website: (http://wwwnc.cdc.gov/travel/). There is a drop-down menu under "Destinations" that lists all global sites by country. By selecting a destination, the traveler will be presented with a great deal of useful information, including travel notices and safety issues, trip preparation tips and recommended vaccines, as well as disease and medication specific information.

Dr. Weil's website (http://www.drweil.com/) has some very useful information about travel-related issues as well, particularly for those interested in an alternative medicine perspective. Ultimately, travelers should make an appointment at a travel medicine clinic **at least 6 weeks before traveling** to get all necessary vaccines, prescriptions, and information.

What prescriptions or vaccines should I get before traveling?

Travel-related diseases and health problems can be categorized into a few simple groups:

- **Exposure Related:** Includes things like the weather, altitude, and contaminated water.
- **Animal Related:** Includes bites and rabies.
- **Insect Related:** Includes a large number of mosquito-induced illnesses (Yellow Fever, West Nile, Malaria, Dengue Fever, etc.) and tick-borne illnesses (Lyme, Rocky Mountain Spotted Fever, etc.).
- **Food Related:** Includes traveler's diarrhea, typhoid fever, etc.

The types of vaccines and prescriptions required before traveling are completely dependent upon where you are going. Exploring the CDC website will give you a good general idea of what may be required for your specific travel plans (including recommendations relating to whether you will be staying in urban areas or going into more rural or remote places), but in the end you will need to visit your travel medicine clinic to get the needed vaccines and prescriptions. After getting your necessary vaccines the most important questions to ask your travel medicine clinician is whether you will need a prescription to: 1) prevent malaria, and 2) prevent traveler's diarrhea.

As a physician comfortable with alternative medicine, I have certainly heard the arguments about not getting vaccines or taking prescribed medicines. After all, not everyone who travels gets ill. While that is true, it is also important to realize that some travel illnesses are life-threatening or deadly. Having treated patients with significant illnesses acquired while traveling, I encourage all travelers to consider the risks of avoiding preventive measures and/or using unproven measures to prevent and/or treat travel-related illnesses. It is also important to keep in mind that not all diseases have vaccines to prevent humans from acquiring them!

What would you take in your personal "First Aid Kit" on a trip? Does it change depending on location?

A great "first aid kit" would consist of the following: **sun block**, **insect repellant** (chemical or alternative), **Imodium A-D** (great for diarrhea, but if it persists you need to take the antibiotic your doctor gave you for traveler's diarrhea), **Pepto-Bismol** (believe it or not, taking two 262-mg chewable tablets four times daily, with meals and once in the evening, can prevent traveler's diarrhea—if you're up for taking the medicine that many times a day!), **melatonin** (as needed when crossing multiple time zones, to help with jet lag, taken just before sleep for the first few days), **probiotics** (if you end up having to use your **antibiotics**, take every day while using the antibiotics), **iodine tablets** (if needing to purify your water and you aren't able to boil consistently) and **Diamox** (an altitude sickness medicine—if going to a high elevation—you need to get this from your doctor). You will notice that the "kit" may have slightly different components depending upon where and how far away you are traveling.

How can someone prevent diseases while traveling?

Prevention is the key when traveling. A few pearls of wisdom: avoid drinking water when you are not absolutely certain of the purity (when in doubt, purify); use some form of insect repellant and particularly mosquito bite prevention methods (use of nets, expose the smallest amount of skin, avoid bright clothing and sweet fragrances on your body—mosquitos might be attracted to these, and use extra caution at dusk) particularly when malaria may be a risk; examine your body for ticks regularly; be careful where you choose to swim; ensure your food is cooked through, avoid raw meats and ensure you wash foods whenever possible. With some extra prevention it may be possible to avoid taking unnecessary medications or visiting a doctor (either overseas or upon your return home).

Similar precautions (as noted above) should be taken when traveling with the elderly or children, in a similar fashion to how you are preventing travel-related illness in yourself. The main differences are that the elderly may be dealing with chronic diseases that require monitoring (blood pressure, blood sugar, etc.) and regular medication administration, whereas children may not exercise the same level of caution or judgment relating to swimming, eating, or drinking. Therefore greater oversight of these activities may be required.

What if I get sick while traveling in a country where most people don't speak the language? Who can I contact in the U.S. to help me?

Some travel medicine clinics offer to provide remote assistance if you get ill while abroad—check with your provider. Consider getting emergency medical evacuation insurance, which is often reasonably priced and can avoid expensive bills in the unfortunate event that you are hospitalized overseas. If your symptoms are concerning or severe you may need to seek care from a local physician where you are traveling, in which case you will need to use your best judgment about the quality of the services provided. You may also want to explore resources through the International Society of Travel Medicine at: http://www.istm.org/.

What illness symptoms are red flags? What should I do about them?

When traveling overseas it is important to keep in mind that every fever is not malaria and every loose stool is not traveler's diarrhea. If you experience any significant symptoms (ongoing fevers, severe diarrhea, dehydration, severe joint pains, unexplained rash or any alteration of your mental state) it would be best to seek the care of a medical professional regardless of where you are located.

Overcoming A Fear of Flying
Alisha Tamburri, Ph.D.

www.clearmindhypnotherapy.com

Alisha Tamburri PhD, CCHT, MH is a clinical Hypnotherapist and counselor with more than 30 years experience. She is also a HypnoBirthing childbirth educator who has guided and advised hundreds of mothers and parents-to-be, including such celebrities as: Alanis Morrisette, Amy Adams, Jessica Alba, Bridget Fonda and Danny Elfman, and also Melissa and Matt LeBlanc. She's also a lover of yoga, almonds and travel.

Alisha Tamburri, Ph.D.

So you're ready to explore new places and venture out of your daily routine by traveling to a place you always dreamed about visiting, but something is holding you back. Something you can't seem to control. Is fear of flying stopping you from living an exciting life?

Don't let it. Your subconscious mind (where fears and phobias stem from) is a powerful thing, but it's also something you can change. By tapping into your subconscious fear of flying, you can reprogram that part of your brain to overcome your anxieties and have that trip you've been longing for.

There are some very simple things you can do to get yourself into a good mental state so you can relax and enjoy the ride. The mind cannot hold two sensations at the same time. We are either stressed or relaxed, we cannot be both. Remember you are in charge of your mind and body. Whatever you tell your body, it will do.

Simple Techniques to Reprogram Your Mind

Emile Coue', born in France in 1857, was a psychologist and pharmacist who introduced a method of psychotherapy, healing, and self-improvement, based on autosuggestion or self-hypnosis. His book *Self-Mastery through Conscious Autosuggestion* caused a sensation upon its publication in England and the U.S. in the 1920s. His familiar mantra, "Day by day, in every way, I am getting better and better" is known as the Coue' Method.

Coue's techniques are used today by repeating words or images as self-suggestion to the subconscious so the mind can be conditioned and then it will produce an autogenic command when needed. Every idea that occupies the mind is transformed into a physical or mental state. What's expected tends to be realized!

Before Your Trip

When you are beginning to establish a habit effectively, you can start programming yourself before falling asleep and several times during the day. This is one of the easiest ways and will only take sixty seconds. You can give yourself a positive suggestion such as "I feel relaxed whenever I'm flying." Every time you say the suggestions to yourself, press down each finger to your thumb, one at a time, on your right hand and then your left hand until you have completed the suggestion ten times. Imagine yourself calm and relaxed on a plane while doing this.

Practicing this technique at night is especially powerful because our minds are very open to suggestions just before falling asleep. As you lie in bed, listen to your favorite relaxing music and envision yourself at your final destination calm and relaxed after a peaceful flight. Tell yourself: "I am peaceful, calm and relaxed. I feel relaxed whenever I'm flying. I will arrive at my destination happy and relaxed." Or choose whatever positive phrases feel most natural to you and repeat them. Say those words to yourself as you imagine them to be so. The mind needs repetition, so the more you do this the quicker it will replace old fears.

Technique #2

Another technique that is a wonderful way to get rid of anxiety is called "Tapping" or EFT, short for Emotional Freedom Technique. It was specifically created for fears, phobias and post-traumatic stress.

The way it works is to say out loud what you are feeling in a sentence such as, "I am afraid of flying," and tapping on acupressure points on the body. Before starting you can give the fear a number from ten being the worst, to zero (it is gone) to see how quickly you can bring down the anxiety level. The tapping serves to release the blockages that are created when a person is in a stressful situation or thinks about one. When the blockage is released the emotions come into balance, creating freedom from fear.

Dr. Mercola's website has a great breakdown and how-to video on tapping at http://eft.mercola.com/

There are also many other free online sites and YouTube videos to guide you through the process. You can tap before and during a flight.

On the Plane

Bring your iPod with your favorite relaxing music or an audio book. You can start listening to it before the plane takes off to prepare you for a pleasant flight. Close your eyes and envision yourself at your destination doing some of the exciting things you want to do. Repeat Coue's method of finger touching and repeating those positive phrases to yourself as soon as you are on the plane. You can repeat this technique as often as needed on your flight.

If you have also been practicing the tapping technique, you can tap as well. Whatever makes you feel the most comfortable.

Professional Help

Many people seek out a professional hypnotherapist who specializes in fears and phobias. You should leave the session feeling at ease and with your own personalized recording to listen to every day and on the plane. Often this can be accomplished in a single session.

When you let go, you gain control. Infinite wisdom resides with you always. Remember you are the master of your mind and body. Happy travels.

Tips for Flying with Surfboards
From Surfer and Swim Coach Rod Samper

http://aquaswimonline.com

Rod Samper runs a premier private swim and lifeguard service in Los Angeles and is a surf instructor to the stars. He is also a close friend, a fellow traveler, and a surf-vacation junkie.

Rod Samper

The sport of surfing has experienced absolutely explosive growth in the last few decades. With this growth and the greater number of surfers has come a problem: crowds. Every surfer would ideally like to have a session with great waves all to himself or shared among a group of friends. This ideal is getting harder and harder to achieve in the more heavily populated areas that most of us reside in. I live in Los Angeles and while I do regularly enjoy the quality waves that can be found in Malibu, Ventura, and other nearby spots, I don't often get to enjoy these waves alone. It goes without saying that uncrowded waves are infinitely preferable to sharing the lineup with 200 of your closest friends. The latter is an accurate picture of first point Malibu on a good swell.

For many the answer to this issue is a surf trip. A vacation centered around surfing is not only great for the experienced surfer but can be fantastic for the beginner as the chance to go to a warm water spot with easy waves and good instructors. This can make for an extremely productive learning experience.

OK, so far so good, so let's grab a board and get on a plane and get in the water. Uh oh … not so fast! Get ready to be shocked by surfboard baggage fees. It's no secret that the airline industry has been charging more for baggage in recent years, but some of the fees that certain airlines charge for boards are just ludicrous. A guy I know just flew to Indonesia for a fantastic trip but China Air charged him $200 per board each way. Since he flew with three boards, this resulted in a total baggage charge of $1200! Mind you, he was traveling with three shortboards. Each was no longer than 6'6" and the whole bunch together including bag weighed less than 35 lbs.

While other travelers can pack light and go minimalistic to avoid excess baggage charges, a surfer may not have that option since without a board our proverbial surfer will spend those precious vacation days on the beach building sand castles and skipping rocks. This could be fine if you are a kid but not if you are a surfer watching a good swell slip through your fingers.

In general, there are two types of surf trips. These are the trip to a lesser known and not as well-serviced destination versus a trip to a more known and better serviced surf destination. The strategies to make the most of these trips vary based on the type, so let's take a look:

If you are contemplating a trip to a well-established and well-serviced surf destination such as Hawaii or Costa Rica or Australia, then you can consider renting equipment at your destination instead of bringing your own. While these kinds of destinations will often be more crowded than the feral, off- the-grid destinations, the advantages of lots of choices of accommodations, guide services, and rental options can make this kind of trip especially attractive for a traveling family, where perhaps your spouse and/or children do not surf. In Costa Rica, one can rent a quality board for $100/week. Hawaii can be similar to a bit more, depending. Since it can cost

$200 each way to fly with a board, renting can save a lot of money.

In most cases when you book a surf vacation, or any vacation, you will do it well in advance and therefore you will not have the luxury of knowing what kind of swell, if any, you will experience on your trip. Many a surfer has been skunked on his or her big trip of the year and dealt with prolonged flat spells. It's for this reason that consistency is prized above all at the premier surf destinations such as the Mentawais in Indonesia.

One advantage of renting boards at your destination is that you can rent equipment only for the days that there is swell. If we look at two scenarios for a hypothetical surfer on a two-week trip to the Tamarindo region of Costa Rica, we can examine how renting boards can save quite a bit of cash. In Scenario 1, let's say our guy wants to take two of his own boards on Delta Air Lines. One board for bigger, faster waves and another small wave board in case there are days that call for that sort of equipment. His two boards will run him $150 each, one way. So that's a total of $600 for surfboard baggage fees. In scenario 2, the same surfer decides to rent boards upon arrival in Costa Rica. Since Tamarindo is a regional surf hub in Costa Rica, there are plenty of places to rent boards and the selection is good. Let's say our surfer arrives to find that the forecast calls for adverse winds and not much swell on tap for the first week of his trip but the models call for some solid swell with clean conditions for most of the second week. This is a very typical scenario. A surf spot would be considered quite consistent if it had decent, rideable surf 50% of the time.

Our guy in this scenario decides to focus on non-surfing related activities such as rainforest treks for the first week and only rents for the second week. He wants a good board so he pays a little more to get a premium board from a rental shop and this runs him $150 for the week. Towards the end of the week the swell is winding down but still is rideable and our man wishes he had that small wave board. He swaps out boards at the rental shop to get something suitable and he finishes out his trip happily. Total cost $150 and he has avoided the hassle of flying with boards, and his own personal boards have not had to run the dreaded gauntlet of the baggage gorillas.

Advanced Tip:

As an alternative to renting, you may consider purchasing a board upon arrival. This will tend to be more feasible only at the well-known and well-serviced destinations. This could be a great option if you are planning an extended stay. Let's imagine a surfer who will be enjoying a two-month stay in Hawaii. If she buys a board on arrival, she can sell it back to a shop at the end of her trip for 50-60% or more of the purchase price. Buying a board for $600 and selling it back at the end of the trip for $400 nets her a $200 board "rental" fee over two months. Not bad. Even if you buy a more expensive long-board you can still end up with a very reasonable cost outlay for your equipment, especially as noted above if your stay will be a long one.

But what if you really want to get away from the crowds? Let's take a look at potential surfboard baggage costs on a surf trip to a more remote destination with less service infrastructure present. The lesser known spots in Indonesia, some of the South Pacific Islands that are a little bit off the beaten path, perhaps the more remote southern coast of Morocco, or even the Northern coast of Chile; destinations like these might have a great deal of appeal to an intrepid surfer really looking to get away from the masses and feel like an explorer. However, board rental possibilities could be slim to none at places like these. If you want to plan a surf trip to the less-explored corners of the surf world you are most likely going to have to bring your own equipment. One's first instinct might naturally be to look at the airlines with the lowest fares to one's destination, but in fact it would be wise to factor in the airline's baggage costs before making a purchase. The airline with the lowest fare to your destination might not have nearly as good a board bag policy as a slightly higher fare airline who may offer to fly your board bag for free. Free? Yes, some airlines are gracious enough to fly your boards with no extra charges albeit with some restrictions in terms of total length and weight. These restrictions are highly individual and can be studied in more detail here:

http://www.surfline.com/travel/boardbag_charges.cfm?id=15425

As you can see, some of the surfer-friendly airlines include: Air New Zealand, Qantas, British Airways, LAN, Air Tahiti Nui, Sri Lankan, Virgin Atlantic, Interjet, and South African Airlines. Some not so good ones are: Cathay Pacific, United, Delta, Iberia, Korean Air, US airways and China Air.

One potentially frustrating but also useful addendum to the above information is that there can be a tendency for considerable variation from the above policies. This can depend on which particular airline agent happens to check you in and that person's mood at the moment and knowledge, or lack thereof, of their own airline's policies. Usually any confusion or ignorance can be worked to your advantage. Example: As you can see from the above, many airlines charge by the individual board rather than by the board bag. If the agents start to check in your board bag with two or three boards in it as one surfboard, by all means let them. Often the airline representatives may be aware of the policy and have an accurate picture of your bag's contents but may reduce the charges if you are friendly with them. Flirting can be a valid option at this point. Some airlines will charge you more if a board bag exceeds a certain length but you can often avoid this sort of charge as well if the ticket agent is favorably inclined towards you and refrains from bringing out the measuring tape. Remember to pack your boards with good quality, padded bags, remove all fins and take extra care to pad the noses and tails of your boards.

Good luck.

Finding a Home Away from Home
A New Perspective from writer Jamie Gambell

http://www.jamiegambell.com

http://www.monkeypipestudios.com

Jamie Gambell was born and raised in South West London, but now lives and works in Los Angeles. He has traveled well, and is well-traveled thanks to a career in film, which included covering sporting events, like The World Cup and The Asian Games. In his spare time, Jamie likes to play Hi-Ho Cherry-O with his son, and write comic books. We've spoken many times about those places in the world we feel akin to. Here's his story.

Jamie Gambell – Roma

"Where are you from?"

I was born in London, England. Even though we moved around a lot when I was a child, it was always within the same borough of London in which I was born.

When people asked me, "Where are you from?" the answer seemed screamingly obvious. I was born there, I was raised there, I lived there—the same South Western corner of London in which my father had spent most of his life.

Some friends had richer backgrounds; born in one country, raised in another, family lines stretching back and further afield— to the furthest corners of the globe; a childhood spent in Australia; a family from the former Yugoslavia; a father from Iraq, mother from Manchester.

"Where are you from?"

I never felt like I belonged, even with my oh-so-exact definition of where I was from.

I have visited Rome several times. Having studied Ancient History at university, I first studied it through textbooks, bringing the Eternal City to life. I found myself fascinated by the descriptions of a city like no other, a place of a million people, living their lives as the machinations of history ground and turned around them.

I had been to Italy before, in High School, but that was to the North, to Venice and the smaller towns around it. Rome always had my eye though.

It was a few years after graduating that I first set foot in the city, which has such a strong draw for me. I stayed just east of the Vatican, in a two-star hotel just off of Piazza Camillo Benso Conte di Cavour. A small place, seemingly more staircase and doorway than hotel—it was perfect.

Having since visited several times, Rome seems to me to be one of those cities, unlike my home town—with its overpriced and under-kept hotels—where there is no bad place to stay.

Rome is one of those perfect cities, too, wherein you can walk in any direction (as long as it is away from the Colosseum) and find fantastic food, matched by the wine. Lying in the center of Italy, it is serviced by the influences of the total country—the heavier, meatier dishes of the North, and the lighter of the South. The seas never being too far from anywhere on the boot, great seafood seemed always available also.

I was lucky enough to spend a long time in Rome when I found myself working on a movie shooting thereabouts. I set up home in a hotel a little further North than the one I had first stayed at, and let myself find my own routines—a certain restaurant on a certain day, a walk South to the Trastevere quarters (a place filled with life and energy and youth and the ancient). Every Sunday I would walk to a pastry shop on the Via Dardanelli, and sip Prosseco and eat small sweet and savory cakes, as the families around me passed through on their way to and from church.

My one bad food experience in Rome came when a couple of friends visited from England, and we decided to check out a restaurant recommended in a guidebook one of them had brought over. As we sat down to eat, I noticed tables of couples and friends, all with the same guidebook. The food was average, the wine worse.

It would be the only time I would use a guidebook to find a place to eat in Rome. Instead I would rely on recommendations—from friends, people I met, a few that I worked with, all would know of at least one great place to go. Gradually my list grew and grew.

More and more, I felt at ease and at home in Rome. Flights were cheap and easy to come by—often one was able to find deals for long weekends, flights and hotels combined, for roughly the cost of a night out in London. I dreamed of living there, of finding a small apartment in Trastevere, and somehow commuting back and forth between England for work, and Rome for life. It was never meant to be, however.

Life decided that I was better placed on the other side of the world—away from the hometown, but also away from the convenience and accessibility my hometown offered me to Rome.

People still ask me "where are you from?" and I still answer London, but I know deep down that I really feel like I'm from Rome.

Special Tips

1. *Whether you're looking to visit one country or multiple countries in Europe, flying into the cheapest city available from your location can save you hundreds of dollars. Then you can take a cheap flight on a smaller airline (or even take a train) to the other cities/countries of your choice.*

2. *If you're flying to Europe and can't find an award ticket to the city/country you want, use your award to fly to the closest city/country to your destination. Then take a cheap flight or a train to the location you want to be.*

3. *When traveling, there are other costs beyond flight and hotel that all depend on your location. If you want to travel longer term or simply want to save money on food, attractions, and adventures while you travel, choose a country where your money goes further. For instance, you could choose to go to Buenos Aires instead of Paris. Everything from clothes, to food, to hotel, to concerts is a fraction of what they cost in Paris.*

4. *When booking a flight within Europe, always search for a round-trip fare. Round-trip fares within Europe are usually cheaper than one-way tickets. Just book the round trip and don't use the return ticket if you don't need it.*

5. *It may seem obvious, but it's easy to forget that visiting other countries during their "off season" can save you a ton on everything from airfare to hotel, to food to attractions ... plus there are fewer tourists!*

6. Taxi-takers beware. Taxi rates can be highly inflated for your benefit as a tourist. Always check with a local at your hotel, a store, restaurant, etc. and ask what the approximate taxi fare would be from where you are to where you are going. That way, you can pay closer to the local rate rather than the tourist one.

7. Don't assume that every country in the world speaks English. There are many countries (like Japan) where you would be surprised to discover just how many people do not, or will not attempt your language. As a sign of respect for the country you're visiting, take the time to learn at least a few key words that will allow you to communicate with the locals of whatever country you are visiting.

8. What can I say? I love basketball. If you like to play and want to know where to find a court while traveling, check out this website www.courtsoftheworld.com. Oh, and yes, there's an app for that.

9. Wish you could combine your British Airways Miles with your spouse's or your kid's? You can, with British Airways' Executive Club Household FF accounts. They are free to set up and can be used by up to seven members of your household as long as they have the same address on file with British Airways. So now those extra 4,000 points you were shy can be taken from another household member's account and bam, you're flying Business Class, baby.

PART 5
Rock Star Travel Accommodations

CHAPTER 13

Where You Stay Matters

"We travel, some of us forever, to seek other states, other lives, other souls."
—Anais Nin

Scoring a free flight to your dream destination can save you tons of money. But many people forget that a hotel stay can cost even more than a flight if you don't use the money saving strategies I write about in this chapter.

After all, a Rock Star Traveler doesn't fly First Class to Paris and then head to the closest youth hostel. I like to travel in style and if you're reading this, you probably do too. I'm sure some folks might enjoy staying in a youth hostel and listening to other people snoring on a cot one foot away from them (if that's you, feel free to skip this section). But if you'd prefer to be sleeping in the privacy of your own suite, in a giant king-size bed, with killer views of the city, and a waterfall shower at your disposal, this section is for you.

It should be noted that no matter what level of hotel you choose to stay in, you should still be getting the best deal possible. I would opt for staying in a five-star hotel while paying two-star prices, which I'll show you how to do in this section, but it's really up to you.

Also, keep in mind that when taking a trip, location can be even more important than the level of hotel you desire. In large cities, many high-level hotels are right in the middle of the action. But beware of the super-high-end hotel with all the bells and whistles at a steal of a price that's just a "train ride" or "cab ride" or "a mile or so" from town. A bargain can become a burden if the hotel is too far from the things you want to see and do. I'd rather sacrifice the level of hotel and be in a good location, than stay in a nicer hotel further away. Remember, your vacation time is valuable and wasting it taking cabs and trains from your hotel to your destination isn't the best way to get the most out of your trip.

Hotel Loyalty Programs

The SPG Le Meridian Hotel in Vienna, Austria, is everything you'd expect with a little Sprockets thrown in for good measure. It is a hyper-modern extravaganza, filled with bizarre yet intriguing art, complete with strange music videos enclosed in giant plastic boxes, a sleek bar that mixes unusual glassware with acrylic chairs, its own little coffee/breakfast shop, a beautiful dining room with glowing floor streaks … and did I mention the colored lights and background sounds of birds chirping in the elevators? It's Wunderbar! The rooms are modern chic with attention paid to every detail. Plus, it's Vienna—one the most amazing food cities I've ever visited. Even late night room service is incredible.

Contrary to what you might think, you don't need to pay a fortune to stay here. In fact, with the right points, you could be staying here absolutely free. Just like the airlines have Frequent Flyer programs (a.k.a. Loyalty programs), so do hotel chains. These programs are your gateway to luxury travel at reasonable prices.

Earning Free Night Awards at Luxury Hotels

When you earn enough Loyalty points with a hotel chain, you qualify for an award booking. The number of points required will vary by the hotel chain and standard of the property.

Every hotel chain has various levels of properties. Obviously, the nicer the hotel, the more points it will cost to stay there. A free night at a St. Regis Hotel will cost more than a free night at the Sheraton.

Hotel Loyalty Programs Also Offer Points + Cash Combo Awards

These can often be a really great deal, as they require way fewer points combined with a small outlay of cash. Last year, I stayed at a Sheraton Hotel in Singapore. It's a four-star hotel with an awesome pool, superb gym, and incredible breakfast and lunch buffets. An average room at this hotel costs $275 USD. But did I pay $275 a night? Of course not. I paid $60 a night using a "points + cash" award (4,000 points plus $60 USD per night). In addition, I got a room upgrade (a benefit of having Platinum Elite Status).

Even if you don't stay in hotels often, it's worth joining their Loyalty programs. Free nights earned occasionally are better than free nights earned *never*, right?

Choosing the Right Hotel Program for You

There are hotels to suit every type of traveler and most of the big hotel chains have different categories of hotels from basic to uber-swank. You need to decide at what level you are comfortable, while realizing that the fancier the hotel, the more costly it will be (either in money or points). Of course, there are ways to save money on all levels of hotel, so let's look at how we can get some serious value out of our vacation dollars.

If your business pays for you to stay repeatedly in a certain hotel chain, you should definitely sign up for their Loyalty program, if you haven't already. Obviously, if you prefer a certain hotel that you frequent, or a hotel chain that has properties in the places you want to travel, those should be the very first hotel Loyalty programs you join.

If you're looking for accommodations and don't know where to start, Starwood, Hyatt, Hilton, and Marriott are known for having good hotel Loyalty programs and having co-branded credit cards that offer great sign-up deals.

Earning Hotel Points

Hotel points are generally earned by:

- **Hotel Stays**
- **Using a Hotel-Branded Credit Card**
- **Credit Card Sign-Up Bonuses**
- **Receiving Elite Status Bonuses**
- **Using Online Shopping Portals**

Hotel Stays

When you stay at a hotel, sign up for their Loyalty program (if you don't already belong to it) and simply enter your Loyalty number when you book your room online or give it to them at the check-in desk. If you travel a lot for business, these points will add up and earn you free award stays when you are on a vacation with your partner or family.

Very Important: *In most Loyalty programs, your stay must be booked via the hotel's own website in order to earn points.*

Some years back, I made a huge mistake booking a stay at the Aloft Chicago via a third party booking engine since it was marginally cheaper than booking on Starwood's own site. By doing so, I forfeited points I would have earned and credit toward Elite Status. Live and learn.

Using Your Hotel-Branded Credit Card

Some of the best credit cards are hotel point earning cards. The Starwood Preferred Guest AMEX is my go-to card for any place that accepts AMEX and it is one way that I earn tens of thousands of points per year. You can read about all of Starwood's benefits in detail at: rockyourtravel.com

Credit Card Sign-Up Bonuses

Of course, just like with airline miles, the fastest way to earn hotel points is via credit card bonuses. Hotels partner with banks and provide credit cards that earn bonus Loyalty points, Elite Status, and free nights.

I'm not going to bore you by going over all that stuff again. But unless you're a super-frequent traveler, getting a hotel credit card is by far the fastest and easiest way to earn free stays and really rock your travel.

Even faster than day-to-day spending with a mileage/points earning credit card are the big sign-up bonuses the banks offer for getting one of their hotel-branded credit cards.

When I got my Starwood AMEX, I earned 30,000 points after hitting the minimum spend. I also got a Starwood Business AMEX and earned another 30,000 points. That's 60k points and it will easily get me a week of free hotel stays at the Sheraton in Rome, Italy, or five nights at the exclusive SLS Hotel in Beverly Hills. SPG has incredible hotels around the world to choose from.

Another example, this time using "Points + Cash":

The Hotel Danieli in Venice, Italy, is a top-tier (SPG) hotel and listed in Travel and Leisure Magazine as one of the top 500 World's Best Hotels. On the days I checked, the lowest standard rate for this hotel was $517 USD. But with SPG's points and cash, you could stay there for a combo of 8000 points + $150 USD. *Yes*, you read that right. You could be staying in a $517 room in Venice, Italy, just mere steps from the Piazza San Marco, for only $150 a night!

Elite Status Bonuses

One of the benefits of having Elite Status with a hotel chain is that you receive bonus points. Instead of the normal one point earned per dollar spent on your hotel room, you end up getting three points or more depending on the program. This adds up fast. When you have top-level status, you also get a welcome gift. One option for the welcome gift is extra Loyalty points, which for the Starwood chain is 500 points.

Online Shopping Portals

Some hotel chains have online shopping portals that work just like the airline shopping portals and earn you bonus miles for shopping through them.

Let the shopping begin:

- Marriott Rewards (www.mrewards.shopmyway.com)
- Priority Club Rewards (www.priorityclubshopping.com)
- Hilton HHonors (www.hiltonhhonorsearningsmall.com)
- Choice Hotels (www.choiceprivilegesmall.com)

For a complete list of shopping portals, go to: rockyourtravel.com

Elite Status with Hotels

The Shinkansen (Bullet Train) pulls into Kyoto Station and we are on to the next leg of our adventure. After grabbing some delicious yakitori, we go downstairs and take a short taxi ride to the Westin Miyako Hotel.

As soon as we step in the hotel, we are greeted and guided to the check-in desk. Upon confirming our reservation, the staff acknowledges my Platinum Elite Status with SPG and informs us that we have been upgraded to a suite. Yes! The Holy Grail of hotel Elite Status benefits.

I've stayed at this hotel before and really enjoyed it, but I did not have Elite Status the previous time and I was in a room that was somewhat older and dated. I'm excited to see what a suite looks like and how it compares.

It turns out the suites are extremely modern and well-appointed. In addition, it is what I can only describe as enormous by Japanese standards. There's a large walk-in closet complete with robes and a full-length mirror. There's a living room area with a couch, coffee table, flat screen TV, and stocked fridge. Then there's the bedroom. A luxurious wood-paneled king-size bed, complete with yukatas (Japanese robes). A sitting table adorned with fresh sake and some

Japanese salty snacks as my complimentary gift sits next to another large flat screen TV and minibar/safe console.

And of course, the bathroom (or I should say "rooms"). There's a marble-tiled toilet room. A marble middle area with large mirrors, and a beautiful sink area ... and then a shower and bath area. The square footage of the bathroom areas alone could amount to the size of some of the other hotels in Japan I've stayed in before.

Needless to say, I'm thrilled with the upgraded room and ready to explore Kyoto. (For those of you staying here, I highly recommend checking out The Kickup Bar, which is a short walk up the hill. It's a rustic-themed bar that has excellent meatball sandwiches and pizza.)

How would you like to book the cheapest room and get upgraded to a suite for free? Check out at 4 p.m. instead of 11 a.m.? Receive complimentary breakfast for two? Get a welcome gift of extra Loyalty points or a local food upon check-in? These perks are the norm for those with Elite Hotel Status.

The benefits of Hotel Elite Status include:

Priority Check-In

Many hotels have a dedicated priority check-in counter. This allows you to spend less time waiting in line and at the front desk.

Guaranteed Late Check-Out

This is one of my absolute favorite perks of Hotel Elite Status. At most hotels, check-out is usually by 11 a.m. I'm not an early morning person and I dislike having to get up at an ungodly hour and rush out of my room before enjoying my morning coffee. However, if you have Elite Status, you can simply call the front desk and request a late check-out and it will instantly be granted. For example, at Starwood Hotels you will have until 4 p.m. to check out. I find that to be quite civilized. Try doing this without status and chances are, the hotel will want to charge you for an extra day.

Elite Reservation Phone Line

Who likes being on hold forever? Nobody. Which is why Hotel Elite Status members get their own special dedicated phone line to make booking rooms and talking with customer service reps a breeze.

Complimentary Room Upgrades
(The Holy Grail of Elite Status Hotel Benefits)

You booked the cheapest room in the hotel, but with Elite Status it's not the room you'll be sleeping in. And if you're top-tier Elite Status, chances are you'll be luxuriating RST style in a fancy suite after being upgraded at the front desk. It's like paying for coach and flying First Class. What's not to like?

Welcome Gift

A welcome gift can be a bonus amount of Hotel Loyalty points, complimentary breakfast, or a local amenity, which varies by hotel. At the hotel my girlfriend and I stayed at in Kyoto, we were given the choice of Loyalty points, or a beautiful bottle of sake and Japanese treats. Although most of the time, I would opt for the points, we decided to splurge and go for the sake. We were not disappointed!

Complimentary Internet

It really gets me that hotels choose to nickel and dime people by charging extra for Internet. I'm talking about fancy hotels that run $200-300 USD per night or more. They could easily add this cost into the room rate and I wouldn't notice, but I find it offensive that they want to charge an extra $10-15 USD per day for Internet in the room. Elite Status allows you to get complimentary Internet, save a bit of money and not be completely irritated by your hotel.

Club Lounge Access with Free Breakfast/Snack

This is no small benefit. If you're staying in a nice hotel in Paris, Tokyo, London, New York, or some other large city, breakfast alone can run you upwards of $30-40 USD per person per day. If you're staying with another person, the savings are doubled, because the free breakfast also extends to another person staying with you. So you *both* get breakfast for free. In addition, Club Lounges often offer drinks and snacks in the afternoon/early evening, which you can also partake of, for free. Quite a deal and delicious too.

**Complimentary Access to Hotel Gym
(Often Costs $20 Otherwise)**

Like with Wi-Fi, I resent paying for a room in a hotel with amenities I can only access by paying extra for them. With Elite Status, you can enjoy the perks of your hotel's gym without paying an annoying fee to do it.

How Do I Qualify For Elite Status?

Like airline Elite Status, hotel Elite Status needs to be qualified for on a yearly basis. Once you earn status it is good for the rest of that year plus the following year and two months into the *next* year.

For example: on June 15, 2012, you earn Gold Status at Starwood. That status will last the rest of 2012, all of 2013 and until the end of February 2014.

If you don't qualify for Elite Status for 2014 based on the number of stays/days from 2013, then your status will no longer be Elite.

The Basics of Earning Hotel Status

You earn and maintain hotel Elite Status by staying at a hotel a certain number of times (5 stays for Hyatt Platinum), or a set number of nights (15 nights for Hyatt Platinum) in a calendar year.

*Remember, for a stay or night to count toward Elite Status, you must book your room via the hotel's own website and not a third party website.

Stays vs. Nights

Whether you spend one night or ten, if you check into a hotel **once**, it's only considered one "stay."

At Hyatt Hotels, for example, you can earn Platinum Status by either having 5 "stays" or a total of 15 nights. So 5 "stays" of 1 night **each** will get you Platinum Status way faster and cheaper than working towards the "nights" qualification which would require staying 15 nights.

Although not always as convenient, focusing primarily on total "stays" can get you to Elite Status in one third the time of focusing on eligible nights.

Do Award Stays Earn Credit Towards Elite Status?

It depends. Award stays at **some** hotel chains count as days towards earning/maintaining Elite Status. Both Hilton and Starwood count award stays.

Shortcuts to Earning Elite Hotel Status

There are a few shortcuts to earning Elite Hotel Status:

1.) Hotel hopping to maximize the benefit of stays vs. nights.

Many people, myself included, will sometimes use a strategy of only staying in a hotel **one day** then hopping over to another hotel nearby to get another qualifying stay. That way, two nights in one city can become two stays instead of just one. This can be a mild inconvenience depending on how far the hotels are from one another. Occasionally, hotel chains will have hotels literally across the street from one another, like Starwood does in Bangkok. When the hotels make it that easy, it's just silly not to take advantage of this strategy.

2.) Hotel co-branded credit cards that confer Elite Status upon the bearer of the card.

Here's a list of some credit cards that give Elite Status for as long as you have the card…plus cards that give a credit of a certain amount of stays/days to make it easier to qualify for status.

- *Chase Hyatt Platinum Card* – This card automatically gives you Platinum Elite Status with Hyatt **for as long as you have the card**. Platinum Status at Hyatt entitles you to: late checkout upon request (2 p.m.), 15% bonus points earned for your stay, complimentary in-room Internet access (about a $15 per day value), and a few other things.

- *Starwood Preferred Guest AMEX (Personal and Business)* – These cards give you two stays and five nights credit each towards achieving Elite Status. It is possible to have both the

Starwood Preferred Guest Personal AMEX *and* the SPG Business AMEX (I have both). This way you can earn a combined four stays towards Elite Status. It normally takes 10 stays to earn Gold Elite Status, but with the two cards it now only takes 6 stays to earn Gold Elite Status. That's almost 50% faster!

- *Citi Hilton HHonors Reserve Card* – This card gives Gold Elite Status for as long as you are a card member. It normally takes 16 stays or 36 nights to earn Gold Elite Status at Hilton. Among other perks, Hilton Gold Elite Status includes free breakfast and free Internet. For big spenders and business owners: $40,000 spent annually will earn you Diamond Status. This card also has no foreign transaction fee.

- *Priority Club Select Visa* – This card gives Gold Elite Status for the entire time you have the card.

- *Chase Marriott Rewards Visa* – 10 nights credit towards Elite Status in addition to Silver Elite Status for as long as you have the card.

- *Chase Marriott Rewards Premier Visa* – 15 nights credit towards Elite Status in addition to Silver Elite Status for as long as you have the card.

As of the publication of this book these cards are accurate, but these things change often, so please check my website: rockyourtravel.com to see the current up-to-date list.

3.) Status matches

Like airline status matches, some hotels will also status match. Call your hotel of choice and ask what their current status match policy is.

4.) Special Promotions

Hotels sometimes run special promotions that allow you to achieve Elite Hotel Status much faster than normal. It pays to keep your eyes open for these and take advantage of them when they are offered.

CHAPTER 14

Booking a Hotel Room

Fernweh (fern-weh, noun, orig. German):
A craving for travel; being homesick for a place
you've never been.

H ave you ever thumbed through the pages of the latest glossy travel mag, drooling at the possibility of vacationing in a villa in Tuscany, a private beach hut on the water in Bali, or the hottest modern hotel in Shanghai, only to have those dreams shattered when you noticed the nightly rate of these hotels? I have. Many times. I'd always wondered if there were ways to stay at these places for less—and there are.

There are three basic ways to get a good deal on a hotel:

1.) Use hotel Loyalty points/airline miles to book *free* nights.
This is pretty straightforward; you earn Loyalty points via the

methods described in Chapter 13 and then redeem those points to get free stays at hotels.

It is actually quite easy to go on the hotel's website and book these rooms. Conversely, if you're having trouble, then call the reservations center, but make sure you have your Loyalty number available and check the amount of miles you have in your account before calling so you know what you can qualify for.

2.) Use Cash + Points Awards to receive steep discounts on hotels.

As stated in the previous chapter, the Cash + Points option allows you to use a combination of Hotel Loyalty points and cash to get a substantial discount on the regular room rate. This type of award allows you to stretch the number of points you have and is often the best value.

If the website doesn't show availability for Cash + Points, it's good to call and double check because some websites (SPG for example) don't always show the availability accurately, and also sometimes they will open availability when the websites show there is none.

3.) Book via a Discount Membership site.

There are private membership-only websites that will send you deals on spectacular properties worldwide. They are *free* to sign up for and the savings can be substantial.

A few years ago, I booked two nights at a four-star boutique Venice hotel, located a three-minute walk from St. Marco's Square, for $167 USD per night total (including taxes). The going rate on the hotel website for that same booking was over $550 USD (without taxes). That's a savings of around 70%. Other comparable hotels in the area were going for $460-550 per night.

To get these savings, sign up at the websites below and you will start receiving emails letting you know when sales are happening. They don't last long so be ready to jump on a good deal. Enjoy living like a Rock

- Tablethotels
- SniqueAway
- Jetsetter
- VoyagePrive

Keep in mind, you won't generally earn Loyalty points or credits towards Elite Status if you book via these websites. However, the huge discounts available can be a good trade-off.

4.) Use TheBiddingTraveler.com together with Priceline's "Name Your Own Price" feature.

By using this feature, you can consistently get 20-60% off your hotel. For those of you who aren't already familiar with Priceline's "Name Your Own Price" booking tool, here are a few things to keep in mind:

- You don't get to pick the exact hotel you stay at. You are shown the hotel **after** your bid is accepted.
- You won't earn Loyalty points, and your Elite Status (if you have it) will not be honored with the hotel you're staying at because you booked the room via Priceline (a consolidator) instead of booking via the hotel's own website. So don't expect room upgrades.
- You need to pay up front. Your credit card will be immediately charged when your bid is accepted.

- The booking is non-refundable and unchangeable.
- You can't request a specific room type. This may or may not be an issue for you and the hotel may be able to accommodate you later after your bid is accepted, but Priceline is not responsible for the room type and will not provide a refund. If you require a non-smoking room, you may want to skip this strategy if a smoking room is a deal breaker.
- In exchange for these limitations, you can receive some serious savings (often starting around 20% and going up to 60% off, sometimes more).

So if you have a problem with any of the above conditions, then this is not the right strategy for you. Personally, I don't use it often, but I know people who do, and who love it, so let's get to it.

In the past, developing a good Priceline bidding strategy required a **lot** of research. Reading up on every hotel in the area, knowing which hotels had how many stars and what the likelihood would be of getting a hotel with bad ratings etc. For the most avid dealmakers with a lot of time on their hands, it could save them a great deal of money. The same could be said for those who were simply willing to roll the dice and see what Priceline came back with. Now there's a new website called, TheBiddingTraveler.com that makes using Priceline's "Name Your Own Price" much easier.

This website will show you what bids have recently been accepted for hotels in the area you want and how to set up your bidding strategy. What's more, it has an automated system to take a lot of the guesswork out of creating your "strategy" for bidding. Just search for your desired city/area, then fill in the prompts and it will make suggestions for you on how much to bid, how to rebid etc. Nothing about this is completely foolproof, but by using this website you will have a much easier, less complicated time getting a good value with Priceline on a room you want.

Alternative Options for Accommodations

When you're traveling, there are alternatives to staying in a hotel. Here are some you may want to consider:

Airbnb.com

Airbnb.com allows you to search and book private homes, apartments, and even boats. People list their property with lots of photos. There are accommodations at every price point. If you're interested in getting more of a local experience in a foreign place, this option may be for you.

Here's more detail from Sean Bonner:

"Clean sheets. Daily housekeeping. Fluffed pillows. Room Service. Staying at a hotel can be everything you want, except when it isn't. Sometimes, especially when staying in a city for a week or more, I find staying at a hotel can make you feel like a tourist when all you want is to be a local. Sometimes you need a home away from home.

In days of old, finding an apartment to rent for a short period of time was arduous, stressful, and worst of all, discouragingly time consuming. And then AirBnB entered the scene and all was right with the world.

AirBnB is a site that lets you rent out a guest room or your entire house, as well as letting you look for places to rent yourself. Specify location (down to the neighborhood), amenities that are important to you (do you need wireless Internet? How about laundry? Or a stove? Or a bicycle to rent? Or ... you get the idea) and you are quickly presented with a map of locations that meet your requirements, as well as the bios of the people offering them and, best of all, any personal connection you may have to them (do you have mutual friends online?). And of course the price they want for the place, which in my experience, beats hotel options across the board.

I recently spent a week in NYC followed by two weeks in Tokyo with my family—in both cities we rented full apartments in neighborhoods with other families for less than the cost of two nights at a nearby hotel."

House Exchange

If you own your own home, or even condo, there are websites that allow you to list your home and search for homes in other countries where the owners are amenable to a mutual house exchange. You stay in their house, while they stay in your house for mutually agreed-upon dates. Now you've got free accommodations and a housesitter to boot.

Overnight Sleeper Trains

This is particularly useful if you're taking a trip in Europe. Simply book a sleeper room on an overnight train and you have combined travel and accommodation into one. With this technique, you could go to sleep in Italy and wake up in Austria. This can often save you money and time while providing a very memorable experience.

Bonus Tip

Although generally not the best value for your miles, you can use airline miles to book a hotel room. This is important to know so you can take advantage of this when you have lots of airline miles but little or no hotel points and you don't want to pay for your hotel. Remember, this game is all about options and doing what works for you and your family. I used this technique to get five nights of free hotel stays in Tokyo earlier this year.

A Few Rental Car Tips

Do a quick search for coupons.
There are tons of discount coupons online for rental cars. Always do a Google search for these before booking your rental. Otherwise you're leaving money on the table.

It is often cheaper to rent from a non-airport location because airport locations generally have the highest taxes.
It's best to check both airport and off-airport locations before booking a reservation.

The Autoslash Advantage
Autoslash.com searches multiple car rental companies to find you the best rate, applies any online coupons to lower the rate further, and continues searching for better rates on a daily basis. If it finds a better rate, it books it for you. You just sit back and reap the rewards.

Autoslash's drawbacks
Not all rental companies allow Autoslash to show their rates (Hertz, Enterprise, and Avis/Budget all opt out). If you need to rent from one of these companies you may want to try rentalcars.com.

One-way rentals are generally higher than when you return the car to the same location you rented from.
This is due to a drop-off fee! Probably about fifty percent of one-way rentals have this fee.

If you don't want to rent a car but need a ride:

Taxiwiz.com
Use this website to check what your cab fare will be in advance. It has many major U.S. cities and also Paris, Singapore, Montreal, Toronto, Vancouver, and San Juan.

Uber
Use the Uber App (available for iPhone and Android) to request a pick-up and Uber will send the nearest driver to your location. You'll get a text with the estimated arrival time and when the car arrives, you'll get another text. Once you're dropped off, Uber automatically charges the credit card you have on file, including tip. So no money needs to be exchanged with the driver.

PART 6
Superstar Techniques

CHAPTER 15

Pro Travel Strategies

"Do we really want to travel in hermetically sealed pope-mobiles through the rural provinces of France, Mexico, and the Far East, eating only in Hard Rock Cafes and McDonalds? Or do we want to eat without fear, tearing into the local stew, the humble taqueria's mystery meat, the sincerely offered gift of a lightly grilled fish head? I know what I want. I want it all. I want to try everything once."
—Anthony Bourdain,
Kitchen Confidential: Adventures in the Culinary

Strategy #1: Fly to Hawaii for Almost 50% Off

This strategy can be used by a couple, two friends, two acquaintances, two strangers, even two enemies! You do, however, need two people to agree to fly on the same plane at the same time to take advantage of this awesome opportunity.

Step One

Get an Alaska Airlines Visa Card. If you have one already then you are ahead of the game and can skip step one and move directly to step two. Do not pass Go.

Step Two

Buy a flight to Hawaii and use your yearly $99 companion fare to get a seat on the same flight for the second person. Yes, that means if you buy one ticket, the second ticket only costs $99! Crazy, I know. You can fly anytime there are seats available, at the height of summer or the dead of winter. The only caveat is that your seats will be in Coach. They used to offer this deal in First Class, but now that policy has changed and they only offer it in Coach. *C'est la vie.* At least you can cry your eyes out in paradise.

Also, both people will earn Frequent Flyer miles on this flight because both flights count as fully paid flights, not as award tickets (which don't earn FF miles). You can take advantage of this very generous benefit once a year as you receive a yearly $99 companion fare. The only restriction is the flight must be operated completely by Alaska Airlines.

Here's an example of the savings you could reasonably expect:

Seattle, WA to Honolulu, Hawaii

On May 8th, I priced nonstop Alaska tickets in Coach from Seattle to Honolulu leaving June 20th and returning June 27th.

Coach: $716.40 each x 2 = **$1,432.80 for 2 people**

Coach with Alaska Companion Fare:

($99 + $11 tax) $716.40 + $110 = **$826.40 for 2 people**
Using the companion fare, the **money saved = $606.40 USD**

Step Three
Enjoy Hawaii!!!

P.S. – This technique actually works for any destination Alaska flies to, not just Hawaii. But seriously, where else would you want to go instead of Hawaii? Don't waste this on a short, inexpensive flight.

P.P.S – In case you have a family of four and you didn't already think of this, both adults could get an Alaska Airlines Visa Card and use the $99 companion ticket to bring one kid each.

Or if you want to leave the kids with their grandparents, you could always go to Hawaii twice in one year and enjoy some alone time. Life is hard. I see tough choices ahead of you.

Strategy #2: Business Class to Paris for Valentine's Day

> *"Paris is always a good idea."*
> —Audrey Hepburn

With its picturesque architecture, charming sidewalk cafes, world-class museums, incredible food, and well-deserved reputation for romance, it's no wonder Paris is the most visited city in the world.

If you have notions of taking your sweetheart to Paris for Valentine's Day, U.S. Airways offers an amazing off-peak award where you can fly from the U.S. to Europe in Business Class for only 60,000 FF miles between January 15th and February 28th (120,000 FF miles for two people).

The normal "Saver" award for this trip is 100,000 FF miles per person. That means U.S. Airways will give you a 40% discount to go for Valentine's Day.

You can also use an off-peak award to fly Economy for only 35,000 FF miles round-trip per person instead of the usual 50,000 FF miles. But why not use this technique to see what it's like to have a cup of coffee in the big leagues. Business Class all the way. You can always go back to the minors afterwards and fly Economy, but at least you'll have a good story to tell.

Of course, if your darling finds Madrid or Rome to be the more romantic destination, the off-peak award can be used to visit other European cities as well.

Note: If you have the miles for a trip like this and you see availability, jump on it. Available award seats for these deals go fast.

Strategy #3: Buying Miles to Get a First Class Flight at 66-80% Off

Buying miles when they're on sale and redeeming them for an award flight, instead of paying for that flight, can be a great way to stretch your dollar and have an amazing travel experience. If you want to travel in First Class without paying full price, you should know about this strategy.

No applying for credit cards, no waiting to accumulate the miles necessary for an award flight.

Earlier this year, I took advantage of one of these offers and now I'm planning on relaxing in First Class on my way to Hong Kong.

The flight I'll be taking would have cost me anywhere from $7,500 USD - $10,000 USD if I'd bought the ticket the conventional way, but why would I do that when I can spend $2,257.50 to buy the FF miles and then redeem them for an award ticket?

Yes, that's right. I bought the miles from U.S. Airways (a Star Alliance member) when they were offering a special 100% bonus on miles purchased. This is a common offer from U.S. Airways. Their miles normally cost 3.5 cents each (plus 7.5% tax), but now with the bonus the price drops to 1.75 cents (plus 7.5%tax). So that's the equivalent of 50% off.

A round-trip First Class award flight from Los Angeles to Hong Kong, my chosen destination, requires 120k FF miles (You can see this on the U.S. Airways Partner Award Chart). So, I made sure to buy 60k and received another 60k bonus. You used to be able to buy that many in one purchase, but now you have to spread it over two transactions. I then called their reservation desk and found available dates that worked for me and now I'll soon be enjoying a trip for 66-80% off the cost of buying the ticket straight out.

In essence, I'm paying $2,257.50 for a First Class ticket to Hong Kong from Los Angeles. For $100 more, I could buy enough extra FF miles to fly First Class to Europe instead (125k FF miles for Europe). Remember, these are tickets that would normally cost anywhere from $7500 – $10,000 USD.

Another great option would be to use my U.S. Airways FF miles to fly Business Class from the U.S. to Australia or New Zealand for 110,000 miles. This ticket would normally cost anywhere from $6,000 USD – $11,000 USD.

A few things to keep in mind:

- Award tickets can be difficult to get on specific dates, so you will need to be more flexible on your travel dates if you use an award ticket instead of a paid fare.
- A paid fare earns miles, while an award ticket does not.

- You should probably only use this strategy if you have a specific award in mind and not just buy miles to stock up your FF account. There are much more powerful strategies to earn miles quickly, like huge sign-up bonuses from credit cards. However, if the offer makes sense, I say, go for it.

Strategy #4: The World On Sale

If you're like me, then the list of adventures you want to have and places you want to go is endless. Picking which place to go next can be difficult. So why not let the airlines pick for you? Well, what I mean is, instead of just choosing a place from your list of "to go" places, choose whichever place has sale flights to get you there. Since you're going to go to many of those places on your list, if you have flexibility in the order you go there, you can save some significant money.

I liken this to shopping for food. You may go to the market thinking you're going to get some fruit. When you get there, you see which fruit is on sale and that's what you go with.

This strategy can save you hundreds of dollars per year and thousands of dollars over time. Airlines are constantly running sales on various locations and if you're willing to be a little adventurous, you can benefit from this.

A fun and easy way to search for tickets that fit your budget is Kayak's explore tool. It's under the "More" tab, or you can just go to: kayak.com/explore. You simply enter your departure city, set the budget slider at the most you want to pay, and a map will show you all the destinations that fit those criteria.

You can do your search by month, by season (summer, fall, winter, spring) or any month. You can even filter by destination and activity.

Strategy #5: One Free International Round-Trip Flight with Hotel Included

Starwood has a little-known promotion called "Nights & Flights." With this option, you can redeem 60,000 Starwood points and in exchange, receive 50,000 airline miles **plus** five consecutive nights at a category 3 hotel. You can also opt to redeem 70,000 Starwood points to get 50,000 miles plus five consecutive nights at a category 4 hotel.

If two people are going on a ten-day trip together and they both use this option, they could have enough airline miles for **two Economy International Award Tickets and 10 total nights of hotel stay for free**, all for a total of 120,000-140,000 Starpoints depending on whether they stay in category 3 or 4 hotels (or a combo).

Strategy #6: Perfecting the Art of the Weekend Getaway

A weekend getaway is a great way to surprise your sweetheart with a fun trip without having to spend a lot of money, plan an extensive vacation, or use up vacation days.

Last-minute weekend fares are the airlines' way of helping you do this. Airlines are constantly monitoring how full their planes are. When flights to certain destinations aren't filling up, the airlines respond quickly by cutting the airfare price and sending out last-minute offers.

It pays to be aware of these deals. Make sure to sign up for the airlines' online deal alerts. Once you've done this, the airlines will send you email offers every Tuesday outlining the discounted fares for the coming weekend or the following one. If you find something you like, go for it.

You could have a lot of fun with this by not telling your sweetheart where the two of you are going, just the types of things you will do and what kind of clothes to pack.

Strategy #7: Round-the-World Tickets

When I was 12 years old, I read the Jules Verne classic, *Around the World in 80 Days*. For myself, and many others, Verne's book would be the first influence to inspire dreams of global circumnavigation.

These days, alliances and airlines make traveling around the world a bit easier by offering Round The World (RTW) tickets. But most people are not even aware that RTW airfares exist, much less how or why to book them.

Let's start with "why?"

RTW tickets are very versatile. You can book anything from a very simple four-segment itinerary (Los Angeles-Auckland-Hong Kong-London-Los Angeles) all the way to a very complex 16-segment tour-de-force that goes through all the continents.

For those who dream of traveling to multiple countries around the world in the span of a year, RTW tickets can be a great asset when compared to buying multiple one-way tickets in order to travel as much. Not only that, but sometimes a RTW Business Class Fare can be cheaper than a simple round-trip in Business from the U.S. to Africa, Australia, or Southeast Asia. The fact that you could go all the way around the world and visit multiple countries instead of just one for the same price or less demonstrates just how valuable a RTW itinerary can be.

In addition to creating the itinerary you've always dreamed about, RTW tickets give you a whole year to complete your travels. Keep in mind though, with RTW tickets you must always keep traveling in one direction around the globe. A caveat to the "one direction" is that the direction is defined by continent so, for example, since Europe is a continent, you can double back and technically travel in the opposite direction *within that continent*. But once you leave Europe to go to another continent (Asia or North America, for instance) you cannot use the RTW ticket to return to Europe.

Having a year to complete your RTW itinerary allows you to break up a RTW ticket into multiple adventures spaced months apart. This is done by using an award ticket (or paid fare) to fly home and then return later to wherever you chose to temporarily stop traveling around-the-world and continue your RTW itinerary.

Things to keep in mind about RTW tickets:

- You must complete all travel within one year.
- Your routing has to start and end in the same country but it doesn't have to be in the same city.
- All three alliances (StarAlliance, SkyTeam, and OneWorld) offer RTW tickets, but due to their larger alliances, OneWorld and StarAlliance are generally recognized as having the best RTW products. I would recommend either of them.
- Several airlines also offer RTW fares: Air New Zealand, Singapore Airlines, and the combo of Virgin Atlantic/Virgin Australia.
- The itineraries offered by the individual airlines are significantly less complex. This can be good or bad, depending on your desires.

- Each alliance and airline has their own rules and regulations governing RTW tickets, so it's good to do a bit of comparison-shopping.

- All the alliances have mileage-based fares, meaning they are priced out depending on how many miles you travel. They have several levels. For example, Star Alliance has a 26,000 mile maximum fare, a 29,000 mile maximum fare, a 34,000 mile maximum fare and a 39,000 mile maximum fare. So it's best to try to get as close to the maximum allowable miles if you are trying to get the most value out of your RTW ticket.

- OneWorld also offers a "Segment" based program. The price is based on the number of continents visited. There is a limit of 16 segments.

- The cost of RTW fares can vary greatly based on the country you start your journey from, even if the itinerary is otherwise the same. This peculiarity can allow you to save a significant amount of money. A business class fare that starts in the U.S. (generally one of the most expensive countries to start in) can cost 25-40% more than if you start your trip in South Korea or South Africa (currently two of the least expensive countries to start a RTW itinerary in). For that kind of savings, if you live in the U.S., it would be well worth it to use an award ticket to fly to South Korea or South Africa or even Japan (another country that usually has a lower cost for RTW tickets) and begin your RTW trip from there.

- Depending on the complexity of your trip, the fare class you wish to travel in, and the destinations you want to reach, the cost of RTW tickets can vary greatly. The average RTW ticket costs anywhere from $3000 USD to $10,000 USD or more.

For the novice world traveler, planning a RTW ticket requires a lot of time, research, and planning. Plus, you should be prepared for a lengthy phone call or two to the airline you are looking to purchase your tickets from.

You can use the links listed below to see sample itineraries posted by the Alliances. Unfortunately, they no longer list the prices for them.

OneWorld Alliance Round the World Info

http://www.oneworld.com/flights/plan-book-online/

Star Alliance Round the World Info

http://www.staralliance.com/en/fares/round-the-world-fare/

After using the above links to plan your itinerary, you'll need to call the airline and speak to an agent to book your trip and pay for it.

Strategy #8: Mileage Runs

A true mileage run is a trip that is taken for the sole purpose of earning the most miles for the minimum price. This entails taking the longest possible legal routing between your origin city and destination city. The destination is irrelevant.

Most casual travelers want nothing to do with taking the long way. We want to get to our destination with the least amount of hassle and time spent on the plane. At this point you may be wondering why anyone does mileage runs.

Mileage runs are generally done to qualify (or re-qualify) for Elite Status or to earn maximum miles for redemption at a later date.

However, you can use some of the techniques of mileage runners to maximize the number of miles you earn on your normal flights when appropriate.

Instead of flying Los Angeles to New York non-stop (4,940 miles round-trip), you could opt to fly Los Angeles to Miami to New York (6,860 miles round trip). Assuming the cost of the flights was the same, you would earn almost 2,000 more miles for the longer routing. This is a basic example. Some dedicated mileage runners will take flights that crisscross the country and have multiple stops.

CHAPTER 16

A Few Final Thoughts

T hanks for coming on this journey with me. I hope the information I've shared with you leads to many memorable adventures.

I wrote this book with the goal of helping as many people as possible make their travel dreams a reality.

I believe travel is essential and should be available to everyone. By sharing this book and its information with others, you can help make that happen.

You can find me online here:

Twitter: @rockyourtravel

Website: rockyourtravel.com

Please feel to email me at: algis@rockyourtravel.com

I would greatly appreciate it if you reviewed this book on Amazon.

Thank you.

Acknowledgements

My dream of sitting in a coffee shop in Kyoto, furiously writing this book in solitude and spending my free time chit-chatting in Japanese with the locals was not meant to be. Instead, I found myself in the heart of Los Angeles living with my sweetheart, Adrienne, and her nine-year-old daughter Lorelei.

Without realizing it, this project was a collaboration from the start. Relying on the advice, wisdom, talent, support and inspiration of a whole network of wonderful people.

Most importantly, thanks to Adrienne, my co-writer and partner in life; without her this book would not have happened. Her tireless efforts to stay cheerful, supportive and help a first-time writer face down the angry demons of resistance to accomplish a lifelong dream, were a Herculean task.

Thanks to my daughter Riley for always brightening my life and inspiring me to be a better person. Thanks to Lorelei for being patient all the times we had to work instead of playing with you. You're a trooper. And next time you get to go to Japan too!

A debt of gratitude to our publishers, Colleen McCarty and Shari Alexander (Expert Message Group), who worked tirelessly with us every step of the way to help make this project a reality.

You guys rock. Thanks also to Scott Williams, Peter Barlow and Christina Honea for making the book look amazing inside and out.

Thanks to Jamie Gambell, Rod Samper, Alisha Tamburri, and Dr. Brett White for sharing your time, energy and individual expertise. You guys are the best. Thanks also to Patrick and Emiliana Dore, Steven Lanza, and Carolyn Sykes for your generosity in sharing your success stories and helping to inspire others to follow your lead.

Thanks to Sean Bonner for being onboard with this project from the beginning and for taking the time not only to contribute, but to give sage advice about how to make the book the best it could be. Looking forward to more coffee hangouts in Tokyo and Atwater.

Thanks to Tim Ferriss for hosting a life-changing weekend in Napa and to the entire OTK group for being a fountain of insight, information, and inspiration.

Special thanks to Victor Cheng for all the personal advice, honest critiques, and incredible support. I hope the book lives up to your expectations.

Extra special thanks to family and friends for all your support in every way: Gary and Sandy Silk, Pat and Em (for going above and beyond), Julie Campbell and Thor Brisbin, Amy Gambell, Michelle Sadeh, Flora and Karina Ablin, Kyle Oliver and Stephanie Johnson, Michael and Katie Luckerman, Paul Mansfield, Glenn Harrell, Cassy Nehring-White, Chris Plough, Brian Schmitt, Krista Stryker, Rusty Rowe, Enrique Altamirano and family, Luther Cowden, Bob Cooley, Garen Gulbenkian and family, Jason and Beth Seaver, Scot Law, Jeremy Charles, Dirk and Marnie Aulabaugh, Kat and Steve Babbitt, Jeremy Swan and the crew at Broken Art Tattoo (Derrek Everette, Matt Soderberg, Josue Acosta and Dillon Eaves).

Resources

- AnnualCreditReport.com
- AwardWallet.com
- FareCompare.com
- Flyertalk.com
- RockYourTravel.com
- Milepoint.com
- MileCalc.com
- myFICO.com
- Ricksteves.com
- Seatguru.com
- Tripit.com

Glossary

Airline Alliances – A group of airlines that form a network and cooperate in coordinating flights on their various airlines to ensure a more seamless travel experience. Alliances also enable Frequent Flyers to get credit for their miles or redeem Awards even if they fly on one of their airline's partners.

"Anytime" Award – Although the FF miles required for this award are double the amount of FF miles required for a "Saver" award, the Anytime Award has the benefit of allowing you to book a seat on any date including dates that may have been blacked out for other Frequent Flyer Awards.

Award – A free airline ticket or hotel stay/night(s) that can be earned through miles, bonuses, or credit card sign-ups. Note: airport and government taxes (and sometimes fuel surcharges) must still be paid on airline award tickets.

Cash plus miles Award – an award that allows you to book flights using a combination of cash plus airline miles.

Cash plus points Award – an award that allows you to book hotel nights using a combination of cash plus hotel points. These are often an excellent redemption value for your points.

Co-Branded Credit Card – A credit card that is partnered with a specific airline or hotel program, which earns miles or points to be used in that program. Some programs allow you to transfer points to their partners. The Starwood SPG card is a good example.

Credit Card Churning – Applying for co-branded credit cards with large sign-up bonuses, meeting the minimum spend to receive the bonus, and repeating the process at a reasonable interval.

Deep Discounted Fares – Some discounted Coach fares have various restrictions (including the inability to upgrade) and earn miles at a lower rate than the actual miles flown or "Flight Miles." This varies by airline.

Elite Status – Airline or Hotel Status earned by flying a set number of miles or fulfilling a hotel stay/nights requirement. Elite Status entitles the bearer to various benefits including upgrades.

Elite Status Matches – When a competing airline loyalty program or hotel loyalty program offers to "match" your current status, granting you Elite Status with them. There are usually, but not always, a few post-match requirements (e.g. flying a certain number of miles that year or having a certain number of hotel stays).

Elite Status Mileage Minimums – If you fly less than 500 miles, you'll still earn 500 FF miles. Most mileage minimums are 500 miles. So if you take lots of short flights, you could be earning more miles than you're actually flying.

EQMs – Elite Qualifying Miles. These are miles that count towards earning Elite Airline Status. Primarily earned by flying, they are often called "butt in seat" miles. Elite Status and class of service bonuses don't normally count towards earning EQMs. Occasionally airlines give double or triple EQM bonuses for flying specific routes or during specific time periods. Some Airline co-branded credit cards give EQMs for hitting a high spending threshold.

FF – Frequent Flyer.

Flight Miles – These are the miles flown and therefore base miles earned (before class, route and/or status bonuses). You can use a flight calculator such as: www.webflyer.com/travel/mileage_calculator/ to find out flight miles.

Full Fare – An airline fare that costs full price and has no restrictions, meaning it can be cancelled or changed without penalty.

Mattress Run – A mattress run is similar to a mileage run in that it is a stay (or sometimes just checking in and then immediately checking out) at a cheap level hotel at an inexpensive rate to earn a stay towards qualifying for/maintaining Elite Hotel Status

Why would anyone do this? Well, it's a way to leverage a little bit of spending for an increase in Elite Status, which can provide tremendous cost saving and comfort inducing benefits while traveling abroad.

Mileage Run – An airline flight or series of flights taken exclusively to gain Frequent Flyer miles with complete disregard for destination. It is based solely on value (i.e. number of miles earned per dollar spent on airfare).

Minimum Spend – The amount you have to charge on your Airline or Hotel co-branded credit card to earn the miles/points bonus. The minimum spend only has to be reached once, not monthly.

RDMs – Redeemable Miles. These miles are redeemable for awards (flights, hotels, vacations, upgrades). They are earned via any mileage earning technique. You can earn tons of RDMs without even flying.

RST – Rock Star Traveler

RTW – "Around-the-World."

"Saver" Award – These are the awards you will seek to book most of the time, unless you have ridiculous amounts of miles. This award is half the price of a "standard" award.

Segment – A leg of a continuous travel trip. When in reference to RTW tickets, it usually refers to a flight as well.

SPG – Starwood Preferred Guest. The Loyalty program of the Starwood Hotel chain.

Stopover – When you stop at a destination between the start and end of your routing. For example, if you are flying from Los Angeles to Paris via London and you stop in London for three days en route to Paris. The length of allowable stopovers varies by airline. Some airlines even allow stopovers on award tickets.

Made in the USA
Lexington, KY
01 February 2015